INNER WHEEL

A History

by

Jay French

Printed in Great Britain by Dixon & Stell Ltd., Cross Hills, Nr. Keighley, West Yorkshire.

Dedicated in Friendship to
all my Fellow Members
because it is *their* story

Author's Note

THIS history does not set out to be a unique or learned work. Neither is it a chronological record or a precise statistical survey, both of which would make dull reading. It is rather a random selection of reminiscences and of informal observations on the meaning and workings of Inner Wheel as a whole, and more particularly of the growth to date of the Association within Great Britain and Ireland.

Presenting the book in three parts, as a trilogy, is considered apposite, for the three are interdependent. In the first, tribute is paid to the Founder and to many Past Officers. In the second, a factual but not, it is hoped, complacent look is taken at how the Association is operating today. What of Inner Wheel in the future? In the third part the question is posed.

Inevitably a book which has taken two years to compile will lag behind to some extent in mirroring the progress of such an ever-expanding movement. A few statements may even now be out of date, but most, it is thought, will stand for a good many years to come. No index is included, for from the format, it will be simple for the reader to find the part which interests her most.

I have been privileged of recent years to have a front seat in the stalls, so to speak, from which to observe and take an objective consideration of passing events within Inner Wheel. It has been an honour to be invited to write of them, but any views expressed are purely personal as obviously the organisation cannot mean all things to all members. The book has been written, *not for instruction,* but for information and pleasure. It is my sincere hope that in its pages readers may find some of both.

Jay French, 1977.

Acknowledgement

The only true acknowledgement it is possible for me to offer to those who have helped in the writing of this history is — the book itself. Without their willing research and communication with me it could not have been produced.

I had hoped to give each one individual mention, but soon found this was going to be impossible, the response to my many queries having been total, and the volume of information voluntarily supplied far beyond my expectations. I trust, therefore, that everyone who has co-operated with me will understand from these words how deeply appreciative I am.

J.F.

Mrs. Oliver Golding in her nursing years.

A Trilogy

'I see the Past, Present, and Future existing
all at once before me.'　　　Wm. Blake.

A**

YESTERDAY

YESTERDAY

In the Beginning

'BEGIN at the beginning,' the King said gravely, 'and go on till you come to the end; then stop.' The wisdom of Lewis Carroll's words in 'Alice in Wonderland' cannot be disputed, but makes the telling of any story sound deceptively simple, for to find, for example, the true beginning of the story of Inner Wheel, would be impossible. It would necessitate entering into the mind and heart, and more particularly, the dreams of one woman. And there is no end, nor ever will be, we hope, to our story.

But — 'Write a history of Inner Wheel,' they said. History though . . .? Let's face it. History sounds stuffy. It is not everyone's cup of tea, far from everyone's pet subject. The way in which History was presented to many of us in school days was not perhaps best calculated to capture or sustain our interest, consisting as it did of having very often to commit to memory lists of obscure monarchs and battles, and even more dull, the dates of them. There has, however, never been a dull moment that the writer can recollect in the history of the Association of Inner Wheel Clubs in Great Britain and Ireland of recent years. Certainly there have been wordy battles aplenty but they, having achieved their objectives, can now happily be forgotten and the dates which have been outstanding in our history are easily remembered for they give pleasure and pride to recall. This then, we trust, readers will find to be History with a difference.

Let us forthwith make a startling start by stating that there is no such thing as history, *per se,* and say with Thomas Carlyle — 'History is the essence of innumerable biographies.' — and go on from there, for surely this is especially true of Inner Wheel, and the biography with which we naturally must begin is that of our Founder, Mrs. Oliver Golding (née

Margarette Owen), and of how in the early nineteen twenties she took the first tentative steps towards forming what was to become one of the largest organisations of women in the world today.

Women are understandably curious about each other's appearance and characteristics. It is one of their endearing and caring qualities, but at a remove of some fifty years it has been difficult to elicit actual details of Mrs. Golding's personality. Regrettably photographs of her are now scarce. Those taken of her in her later years show a somewhat stern exterior and formidable presence which we know from reading letters written by her and speeches made by her, belie the gentler and humorous side of her nature.

What we do know of her for certain is that she was born in the town of Hay-on-Wye and was of Welsh extraction. She trained as a nurse and served as such during the first World War. It may very well be that her years of service in the nursing profession triggered off a deep desire in her to help all ailing and deprived humanity. It certainly is safe to assume she was not so much concerned about the liberation of women as about giving women the opportunity to liberate others from sorrow and suffering, nor from the outset it seems was she content to see this ideal confined to her own immediate community. Obviously she envisaged a movement embracing a much wider spectrum, but that the organisation she was responsible for founding was to become nationwide to the extent that it has, would, we are sure, have thrilled her. That later it was to span the world so widely, she would, we think, have found incredible.

Philanthropic then our Founder undoubtedly was, but equally a shrewd business woman. When World War I was over she joined the firm known as the 'Nurses' Outfitting Association Ltd.', in Stockport. This was a company run *by* nurses *for* nurses which had been started in 1900 by two women, a Sister Eva Carter and a Nurse Jessie Simpson. In 1919 Mrs. Golding succeeded Sister Carter as Managing Director of the company, a post she held until her death. On each of the firm's brochures, above her signature, the words — *'I personally supervise the making of your uniform.'* always appeared — proof indeed of Mrs. Golding's business acumen and integrity. The firm still exists today, and although now it has merged with others and has moved from its original humble premises to a new factory, it is still in the town of Stockport, and incorporated in its name is the word 'Danco' which it is stated by some to be derived from 'Doctors and Nurses Complete Outfitters' — the trade name of the old firm.

Mrs. Oliver Golding was then — a nurse; a successful business woman; and she was the wife of a Manchester Rotarian, this last qualification indisputably the most important for all that was in time to follow. A Manchester Rotarian . . . ROTARY. Mention of the word brings under scrutiny the embryo of Inner Wheel. The origin of Rotary is simplicity itself to explain. All the world knows of Rotary today, and of how it was the brain-child of a certain young American business man, one Paul Harris of Chicago. There in the year 1905 he formed the first Club, and initially, before any organisation was envisaged, members held weekly meetings *in rotation* in their own homes — hence the name and the adoption of a wheel as emblem eventually followed. It is doubtful if Paul Harris ever heard Disraeli's comment — 'The world is a wheel and it will all come round right,' but it is certain he would have approved the underlying and hopeful message in the words.

The growth of the Rotary movement in the past seventy years has been astronomic. There are in the region of three quarters of a million Rotarians at the present time and the magnitude of the contribution made by Rotary to society world-wide cannot be measured. From the inspiration of one young man, thus illustrating the power of the individual, has come into existence this tremendous organisation, membership of which demands the highest standard of professional conduct and concern for humanity. Sir Winston Churchill said — 'All great things are simple, and many can be expressed in a single word. Freedom; justice; honour; duty; mercy; hope.' Likewise everything about Rotary is simple and straightforward. It sums up in its motto all it asks of its members in three words — SERVICE ABOVE SELF. No one today needs to ask 'What is Rotary?'. Because of its endeavours it is known.

Not yet nearly so well-known is Inner Wheel. Constantly the question is still put — 'Just what *exactly* is Inner Wheel?' and it is not sufficient nor indeed accurate to reply: 'We are the wives of Rotarians' for all wives of Rotarians are not necessarily members of Inner Wheel. All Rotary Clubs do not have corresponding Inner Wheel Clubs (as yet!). And here it is perhaps appropriate to point out that the only correct title for a Rotarian's wife or indeed any female relative who is eligible for membership, is simply — 'A Member of Inner Wheel'. The name 'Inner Wheel' though apt for the organisation, it must be confessed has led to difficulty in finding any short name for the individual member. It led to the Association President, Mrs. T. H. Gameson, admitting in 1950 that she had received innumerable requests to remind members not to use such titles as 'Inner Wheelians' or 'Inner Wheelers'. It led in 1958 to a 'Short-name' competition being held among members, but although many suggestions were submitted none were judged suitable.

And so to trace the name 'Inner Wheel' back to its origin. For many years prior to 1924 when we really start our history, wives of Rotarians in many cities and towns throughout the country, prompted by a concern for public welfare no less than that felt by their husbands, had been voluntarily, in the background, giving of their time and energies to help in any service which was being undertaken by their menfolk. It was only to be expected after all, that they would feel sympathetic to their Rotarian husbands' ideals and wish to contribute. Some formed committees and inevitably some of those committees began to meet at regular intervals and in some instances actual clubs of Rotary wives came into being.

But in which town did 'Inner Wheel', as such, really start? Controversy on the subject has rumbled in the background from time to time with admittedly some foundation, but perhaps it should be borne in mind on this score that ideas have legs. At certain points in time, in the air, born of existing social exigencies or from the impact of those on the individual mind, purposes emanate, and it could well be that, in the early nineteen twenties when the social climate in this country was for many materially poor, into the minds of womenfolk all over who were not particularly deprived, came compassion and a desire to express it. Being the first in anything is after all rather an accident of time, place, available resources and support, so that to cavil on the point is purposeless. Liverpool, Manchester, Bristol, Wick, Timbuctoo. What matters? Without the very first of our members it is true we certainly would not be in existence today. Equally, without the most recently enlisted ones we definitely will not exist tomorrow.

So it is we find ourselves where a group of ladies, much encouraged by their Rotarian husbands came to a decision to call a meeting for the purpose of setting up a club on Rotary lines — the year 1923; the date November 15th; the time 3.30 p.m. and the place, Herriot's Turkish Baths in Deansgate, Manchester. A curious first meeting place it would seem and when on investigation it transpires the meeting was in fact held in the cooling room of the baths, it becomes more curious, but the explanation is commendable. On being asked much later why such an extraordinary choice of venue had been made Mrs. Golding was to admit naïvely that it had been the only room they could get for nothing!

It appears from the carefully preserved Minutes of this meeting that twenty-seven ladies attended. The ladies responsible for convening the meeting explained that the object of such a club as was envisaged was twofold, firstly to foster friendship among the wives of Rotarians and secondly, it was thought, that organised into a club, they could offer much more in the way of service. In the discussion which followed questions were raised as to what form the activities of such a club would take. Many suggestions, it is recorded, were forthcoming, all of sound worth. Evidently, however, at this point, attention was drawn to the fact that there was anything but a full representation of Rotarian wives at the meeting and a decision was taken forthwith to set up a *pro-tem* committee whose job it would be to contact wives who had not attended or had been inadvertently overlooked when invitations had been sent out, also to arrange a further meeting and find a venue for it. Elected to be Chairman of this committee was Mrs. Oliver Golding; to be Secretary Mrs. W. A. Nixon and this is the first time we hear, linked together, the names of these two women who were destined to play the leading roles for many years to come in the founding of Inner Wheel.

The next meeting was called for January 10th, 1924. It was held in the Social Club, Lower Mosley Street, Manchester, and marked the actual commencement of the movement, and for newer members who may have wondered why January 10th should be the one day in the year when it is suggested some special service should be given, this is the answer.

Enthusiasm amongst the ladies concerned had not waned in the short interim period between mid-November and early January. They had not been idle and we read of funds raised and children's woollen garments made and sent to local hospitals, and surely this is the origin of our now well-established practice of producing 'Baby Bundles' sent today to deprived communities all over the world and for which appreciation was expressed as recently as in 1974 by Mirian Dean on behalf of the Dalai Lama of Tibet.

From the records of the meeting we discover Mrs. Golding in the chair, known now as 'President', her suggestion adopted that the Club be henceforth called the '*Inner Wheel* Club of Manchester', and so we hear first ever mention of the name, a name which obviously had been arrived at after much thought, for it cleverly indicates the Rotary connection.

The rules laid down that day were six in number and disarmingly simple. Reading them today gives occasion, on the financial side, to a wry smile. 'Annual subscription to be one guinea, with the option of raising if necessary.' It has indeed been necessary. Having settled on the name and subscription it remained only to say that (a) membership was to be confined to the wives and womenfolk over 21 years of age of Rotarians, present or past of the Manchester Club; (b) that those who lived at too great a distance from Manchester to attend meetings were to be Associate Members at half subscription rate; (c) that meetings were to be held fortnightly, and (d) that meetings would continue throughout the year.

These basic rules were adopted with slight variations by all later Inner Wheel Clubs right up until the advent of the formation of the Association in 1934. Moreover, it was laid down then that the officers of a Club would be the President,

Secretary and Treasurer and that a committee of six would be asked to form, which number is still used at the present time.

The establishment of this first ever Inner Wheel Club was something accomplished but as it was to turn out just the first small step in progress as far as Mrs. Golding was concerned. The Manchester Club never looked back. Within less than a year the membership had more than doubled. If they had problems it does not show, for taken at random from the Minutes of meetings within that first year are references to many successfully accomplished projects, especially for local hospitals, not surprisingly when we recall Mrs. Golding was a nurse. From the outset too it clearly was not a case of all work and no play for many are the whist drives and purely social occasions mentioned. What is more, at the year's end the Club had in hand a substantial sum, by standards of the time.

News of the formation of the Manchester Club and its achievements began at once to spread. Rotary wives in other areas became interested, expressed a wish to follow suit and many contacted Mrs. Golding. Now, as members who have taken any hand in subsequent extension work will agree, it is a demanding task. It calls for a marriage of enthusiasm and tact, the ability to put ideas over convincingly and an industry in letter-writing, the last not everyone's favourite form of pleasurable employment. Luckily for us, however, Mrs. Golding possessed all those qualities. As enquiries from all over the country reached her she assiduously undertook a prodigious amount of correspondence and began to travel widely, giving talks to both Rotarians and their womenfolk. Success crowned her efforts and by 1927 five more Clubs had formed; at Liverpool, Macclesfield, Nelson, St. Helens and Warrington. Not all of those, however, it must here be emphasised, started then from scratch. Far from it. Indeed in the city of Liverpool there had existed since 1916 a Club known then as 'Rotary Ladies' which already had a considerable record of service to its credit. (See 'Going Nationwide' No. 18 District.)

It was in the spring of the following year that a feeling began to manifest itself that there ought now to be some form of unification for existing Clubs, and with this end in view, the ladies of the Manchester and Liverpool Clubs got together. The Rotary District No. 5 Conference was about to be held in Llandudno, and on being approached, the Executive Committee of it was found to be sympathetic to the idea of a Ladies' Meeting being held there to consider the possibility of an Inner Wheel District being formed corresponding to that of No. 5 District of Rotary.

At the meeting of Liverpool and Manchester ladies which was held in Liverpool, Mrs. W. H. Harris of Liverpool was elected Chairman of a *temporary* joint Committee, its function to arrange for a Ladies' Meeting to be conducted during the Rotary Conference. When this meeting took place Mrs. Harris was in the chair and Mrs. Golding was the Speaker, and as far as can be ascertained, it was at this point the first District Committee was established, known to begin with as the 'Inner Wheel Joint Committee No. 5 District Rotary Area.' Soon, of course, this was sensibly curtailed to the 'No. 5 Inner Wheel District Committee', the designation subsequently taken by the Committees of all other Districts as they formed, each using its appropriate Rotary number. Thereafter a *permanent* Committee came into being, this in 1929 and now with Mrs. Golding as its Chairman, and once again the rules laid down were few and straightforward, consisting of the following broad outlines —

That the area administered by a District Committee lie within its corresponding Rotary area; that the Committee be responsible for seeing to it that Clubs carried out the rules laid down for them; that the aim of the District Committee was to unite all Clubs in furthering Rotary ideals; to co-operate with any other District formed; to try to form new Clubs within a District's boundaries and to show friendship throughout.

That District administration followed that of Rotary District procedure was taken for granted. The business would be conducted by a Committee of two delegates from each Club, three if the Club had a sufficient membership; officers elected by ballot and decisions arrived at by vote.

It was then, to the kindly co-operation and encouragement of the Rotarians of District 5, that in 1928 we owed the formation

Association of Inner Wheel Clubs

GREAT BRITAIN AND IRELAND

This is to Certify that the Inner Wheel Club
of *Manchester, 5.*
District No. 5.
having accepted the Constitution
Byelaws and Club Rules of the
Association of Inner Wheel Clubs is
admitted to Membership of the Association

Signed. President *Margaretta Golding –*

Hon Sec. *Gladys M. Nixon*

Date *1st July 1934.* Founder Club

The first Inner Wheel Charter ever to be presented —
MANCHESTER, NO. 5 DISTRICT.

International Inner Wheel

This is to certify

that the Inner Wheel Club of

Llantrisant

District No. 15

Great Britain and Ireland

having accepted the International Constitution
and National Byelaws
is admitted to membership of
International Inner Wheel

Signed *Gwen Barnes*
International President

Irene J. Kerr
National President

Date of formation 12th January 1976

Date of registration 22nd January 1976   Club No. 1980

The Thousandth Inner Wheel Charter to be presented —
LLANTRISANT, NO. 15 DISTRICT.

High Leigh Conference Centre, Hoddesdon, Herts.

(Photograph by Bishop Marshall)

of the first Inner Wheel District. From the beginning they had been casting a benevolent eye on the project of Inner Wheel but it seemed in this particular year that they really came to see the possibility of it becoming a nationwide organisation. Accordingly they went to the trouble of noising abroad among their fellow Rotarians in other parts of the country what was happening and the upshot was that the future of Inner Wheel was given considered attention by R.I.B.I. (Rotary International in Great Britain and Ireland) which body decided not just to lend their ear and sympathy but practical aid. This took the form of permitting the ladies to hold a meeting of their own during the R.I.B.I. Conference at Harrogate that year. To this Mrs. Golding was invited and there put the ladies present into the picture about the Manchester Club's activities. This encouraged others to give accounts of the work which they undertook as Rotary wives in their own home towns.

Beyond any shadow of doubt this opportunity served to spread the glad tidings of what was going on and brought many Clubs into the fold more rapidly than anything else could have done, had the ladies been left to go it alone. A husband's approval in the home is always treasured by any wife. To have his backing and blessing on her interests outside of it is something else again, recognition of her as a person and a sure-fire incentive to her to make a go of whatever it may be. So it was that many were the wives who returned from that particular R.I.B.I. Conference wildly enthusiastic about setting up similar clubs to the one in Manchester. Indeed the plain fact is that, from then on, R.I.B.I. Conferences stand out in our history like giant stepping-stones, for at each of them for the next twenty years a ladies' meeting known as the Inner Wheel Business Meeting was conducted and at almost every one of them, apart from the enormous enjoyment of the social contacts made, seeds were sown which promoted growth and advancement towards national unity.

In 1930, for instance, at the R.I.B.I. Conference in Edinburgh, at the Ladies' Meeting held in the Usher Hall, Mrs. Golding called for more Clubs to form (there were thirty-five of them by then); and a resolution was passed on that same occasion saying that henceforward all to form should be known as 'Inner Wheel' Clubs. This had the immediate effect of several changing the names by which up until then they had been locally known, such Clubs as both Bexhill and Canterbury which had been in existence since 1924; Guildford and Clapham since 1926 and Colchester and Bristol since 1927.

Then again, in 1931, this time at the R.I.B.I. Conference at Llandudno (Clubs now numbered fifty-six) at the Ladies' Meeting in the Town Hall, Mrs. Golding appealed for the formation of more Districts. Consequently by the end of the following year four new Districts had come into being. Three more formed within 1933 and now, although, of course, it had been in the minds of many members as a possibility for some time, was heard the first whisper of some sort of central organisation becoming operational.

It would appear from old records that the initiative in this connection was taken conjointly by members of the newly-formed No. 12, No. 13 and No. 14 District Committees. Their feeling was that it was fast becoming necessary to get more organised conditions if the vast number of Clubs now springing up all over the country were to be kept together. They met in Carpenter's Restaurant, Clapham, to discuss the matter, agreed the setting up of a central body was desirable and accordingly a resolution to this effect was sent to Mrs. Golding in order that discussion could take place on it at the Ladies' Meeting at the R.I.B.I. Conference in Scarborough in 1933.

There the proposal met with approval. A central organisation was to be formed consisting of, at least, a President, Vice-President and Secretary, the Committee to consist of the Chairman and Secretary of all the District Committees. The representatives from each District were elected. They in turn elected Mrs. Golding as President and Mrs. Nixon as the Secretary of an interim Committee which was empowered to draw up a Constitution and By-Laws within the year. Their deliberations took place in the heart of District 13, in the Euston Hotel, London, where Draft Rules were prepared for presentation to the next Inner Wheel Business Meeting.

The year 1934 saw the R.I.B.I. Conference held in Douglas, Isle of Man. It was to be the most momentous and triumphant occasion yet for Inner Wheel, for on May 6th the Constitution and By-Laws together with the title 'Association of Inner Wheel Clubs Great Britain and Ireland' — all was put before the ladies gathered there, was approved by them and ratified, seventy-nine Clubs from the now eight existing Districts having discussed all aspects thoroughly during the preceding year. As was only fitting, Mrs. Golding it was who was elected as the Association's first President and Mrs. Nixon to the office of Association Secretary — 'And it delighted us that this occurred on, as it happened, Mrs. Nixon's birthday' — wrote a member who was present.

Only ten years had passed since the birth of the first Club and now the Association as we know it today was fact. Progress indeed, and fortunately for Inner Wheel progress within it has never appreciably slowed down. Readers will have noticed how the total of Clubs had risen to seventy-nine prior to the formation of the Association. These '79 ers', as they are affectionately referred to today are considered special and rightly so. Particulars of their histories, their present state of health, their activities and interests are zealously preserved, kept up to date and housed in a special card-index at Headquarters.

It was in 1936 that the decision was taken to mark the occasion of a Club's formation by the granting of a certificate of membership (what we now call a Charter) and those presented to the seventy-nine Clubs formed before the Association itself bear the words 'Founder Club' in the bottom right hand corner.

So some of the early Clubs have fallen by the wayside . . . It could not have been otherwise with the exigencies of war and the passage of time. It is indeed remarkable that the 'casualties' have been so few, and on perusal of the histories of Clubs forced to disband, it would appear the fault has not been one of internal conflict but rather of external pressures. In many cases disbandment can be directly attributed to the fact that daily our society becomes more fluid. City boundaries spread. Homes become commercial premises. Areas become depopulated and business people, Rotarians included, find themselves posted from one region to another more frequently than ever before, or for that matter, move on retirement out of the area where they have been in business, so that it can very well happen that members joining one Inner Wheel Club in a matter of months discover their circumstances take them to some other part of the country. It is inevitable. The majority of the '79 ers', however, soldier on with continuous records of service to their credit.

And now we move further into the year 1936 when several things of note happened. By now Mrs. Golding was proudly wearing the Presidential Badge and Chain of Office. R.I.B.I. President F. W. Gray had invested Mrs. Golding with this at the first Inner Wheel 'Business Session' during the R.I.B.I. Conference at Harrogate in 1935. All Clubs had contributed to the purchase of it by a gift of five shillings per Club. It had been agreed that the cost of it was not to exceed £20. The Secretary had submitted four designs and one had been chosen, and for the benefit of members who have not had the opportunity to see this badge close at hand, it is a thing of great beauty. It carries the name of the Association and on it, delicately wrought in enamel on gold are replicas of the national flowers; the rose of England; the daffodil of Wales; the shamrock of Ireland and the thistle of Scotland. Having been re-elected to serve a second year Mrs. Golding was now granted the title of 'Founder President' with the privilege of attending any meetings of Council, District or Club in an advisory capacity. With no thought for herself and tirelessly working for the promotion of the movement she was now travelling up and down the country as never before, chairing and addressing meetings and inspiring others to follow her example. Even if Inner Wheel had been her only interest which it definitely was not, for at this time she was in fact the National Secretary of the Union of Soroptimists — all this effort was bound in the long run to take toll of her health and strength, and unhappily it was beginning to do just that.

A typical day in her life at this time was the April one in 1936 when she travelled from her home to the first Rally to be held by No. 13 District, there in the Rembrandt Hotel, Kensington, to deliver the principal address and present no less than twelve new Clubs with their Charters. In an account of that eventful day we read and marvel at the way in which she had with great care and forethought prepared short, witty remarks and comments appropriate to each Founder President, calculated to encourage and inspire them. She did her homework with a vengeance did our Founder! It commands our total respect.

In her address on that particular day she made too, several pertinent observations which still hold good. She stressed that all Clubs were self-governing; that the service they give is entirely their own affair; that every member is a potential Association President; and she urged members to take office when asked. The work of any officer was *easy,* she declared, if the officer was backed by her Club and in the same speech she expressed the hope that one day she might attain her 'century' — her hundredth Club — and happily she did see that come to pass.

By this time members everywhere were deeply conscious of the great debt they owed to this remarkable woman. Was there no way in which they could in some measure reward her? Of course, there was not. Nothing could really repay her for the opportunities she had given them for service and for the many friendships they had made. Yet it was strongly felt that some tangible token should be presented to her and so it was decided to ask for a small sum per member towards the purchase of a suitable and personal gift, the sum in fact was one shilling. Willingly this was forthcoming and with the money there was purchased the beautiful diamond and sapphire ring which is proudly worn to this day by each successive Association President of Inner Wheel in Great Britain and Ireland.

This ring, together with a wheel-shaped blue and gold leather book, giving the names of the Interim Council for 1933 and the Councils of 1934 and 1935 was presented to Mrs. Golding on Sunday, May 2nd, 1937 at the Inner Wheel Annual General Meeting at the R.I.B.I. Conference in Bournemouth. A report of the presentation in the No. 13 District Bulletin of the time tells us that Mrs. Golding appeared greatly touched, but sadly the first indication that she was now failing in health appears in the same report, for it ends — 'We all hope and pray Mrs. Golding may be speedily restored to health. Her courage and determination to carry on must spur us on to do great things for her sake.'

To breathe first life into a movement destined to become world-wide, to nurture it during its infant years, iron out its teething troubles, guide it through all formative stages and live to see its firm establishment was then what Mrs. Oliver Golding did for Inner Wheel and when one — meaning all of you who are reading this and I who am writing it — pauses to look back on the countless happy days spent in Inner Wheel friendship, reflect on all it means in our lives, when we count — if we can — the many true friends we have whom otherwise we may never have met, when we consider the widening of interests membership has brought us, only then do we glimpse the enormity of the debt we all owe to our Founder who died in the spring of the year 1939.

As can be readily appreciated the tributes to Mrs. Golding's life and work made by members over the years have been many, but perhaps in a work of this size, we may be forgiven for confining ourselves to brief mention of the first and the most recent. On April 19th, 1940, a commemorative luncheon was held in Manchester after which members proceeded to the Memorial Hospital in Stretford which was where Mrs. Golding died and there an inscribed tablet was formally presented. A great deal of money had been subscribed, and bearing in mind the Founder's intense concern for the welfare of nurses, this was used to purchase items of furniture for their comfort in their private quarters. The most recent tribute commemorates the formation of the first Inner Wheel Club and takes the form of a handsome teak seat bearing a descriptive plaque. It was presented to Mrs. Golding's birthplace, the town of Hay-on-Wye by members of District No. 15 in 1975 and stands outside the town library.

Lest it be thought we dwell at too great a length on what this one woman accomplished, and be accused of attributing to her solely the work involved in those early days, we hasten to amend any impression that Mrs. Golding, although undoubtedly the prime mover, went it alone. She was encouraged on all sides, on one occasion by no less a person than Paul Harris himself, who in conversation with her expressed

24

himself 'as being well-disposed towards the concept of Inner Wheel as an International movement' which comment may interest Rotarian readers (if any!) and must have given Mrs. Golding enormous satisfaction. She was exceptionally fortunate too, in that she was surrounded and supported by the right people, in the right places and at the right time, a rare circumstance. Names from the past and names of many still actively with us spring to mind immediately. We hesitate to label them 'pioneers' which sounds pretentious. Rather they themselves would, and do modestly say, that Mrs. Golding inspired them; the idea of Inner Wheel appealed to them; therefore they worked to further its aims. They should not go unsung, and so we proceed to *NAME BUT A FEW* —

The work, for example, of an able and enthusiastic secretary can never be adequately acclaimed and here Mrs. Golding was truly blest to have as her right-hand man from the very first, **Mrs. Gladys Mabel Nixon.**

Indisputably born not made are secretaries of the calibre of Mrs. Nixon. Those who knew her say unreservedly that she was *the perfect secretary,* the backroom girl who shouldered all the humdrum routine work, sought no recognition and shunned the limelight. This last is certainly true, for however thorough the searches have been in old albums, no photograph of her has been found and even biographical data has been uncommonly hard to come by.

So what do we know of this woman whose signature appears so frequently in old records? She was born in the year 1889 and married William Alfred Nixon, an accountant by profession and a prominent figure on the Rotary scene of the time. He was, in turn, President of the Rotary Club of Manchester, Chairman of Rotary District 5 and a Director of Rotary International.

Mabel herself — she preferred to be known as 'Mabel' — was, as we already know, a Founder Member of the Manchester Inner Wheel Club and its Founder Secretary. In 1927 she became that Club's President. When District No. 5 was formed she was its Founder Secretary and in 1935 was appointed Founder Secretary of the Association which office she held until 1939 when illness forced her to resign. Although she never again actually took office at any level her interest in Inner Wheel never for a moment waned and she remained a very active member for many years.

The war years brought her great personal loss. Her husband died in 1941 and his business premises were totally destroyed by enemy action. It is on record that, about this time, as a small token of gratitude for her services to the Association, Mabel was presented with a typewriter. She was deeply interested in the work of the Y.W.C.A. In this organisation she again became a secretary — this time to the organiser of work for the Services in Lancashire who, writing of her at the time of her death, said: 'Mabel was the most efficient and most helpful secretary I ever had. All the staff loved her. She had the most wonderful knack of smoothing out problems for them.' A like sentiment appeared in the District No. 13 Bulletin: 'Mrs. Nixon was unequalled at soothing ruffled tempers of which there were many in the early days — and of reconciling divergent opinions to the common good of the Association, in the doing of which her unquenchable sense of humour played no small part.'

These tributes were paid to Mabel Nixon long ago and were concerned primarily with her ability as an administrator but as recently as in the spring of 1976, written astonishingly enough within weeks of each other, both by members now in their late eighties who lived then in widely separated parts of the country, and unknown to each other, have come personal, interesting recollections of the *woman herself*. Mrs. Ethel Rutter, Founder Chairman of No. 18 District, remembers her in these words: 'She was a wonderful helpmeet and friend to Mrs. Golding. Agreed some members did not admire her forthrightness and obvious reluctance to suffer some suggestions gladly, but she gave hours and hours to Inner Wheel. I admired and enjoyed knowing her.' And Mrs. R. Gordon Bradley, who was No. 13 District Chairman in the early years of the Second World War, had this to say: 'After a severe illness Mrs. Golding was reduced to a tiny frail little person and had it not been for Mabel Nixon who accompanied her everywhere she could not have carried on as long as she did.' To be remembered so is to make it abundantly clear that in

26

Mabel Nixon Inner Wheel had the most valuable vanguard.

Nor did she confine her contribution to the administrative side of things. She was possessed of other gifts, other talents. She was an extremely competent car driver in days when there were not so many women drivers around and so could act as nurse/chauffeuse/companion on the many long, cross-country journeys which were necessary for Mrs. Golding to make. Artistic too she must have been, for it was she who designed the President's ring, cleverly adapting it from a brooch owned by Mrs. Gladys Young of Canterbury, and that the ring after Mrs. Golding's death did not disappear from the Inner Wheel scene was entirely due to Mabel Nixon's generosity, for with foresight and loyalty to Inner Wheel she negotiated to become its owner and subsequently in her will bequeathed it to the Association for all time.

The only recreation Mabel Nixon ever permitted herself in a crowded life of voluntary work was the game of golf at which she displayed considerable skill. (It is rather difficult to imagine when she managed to fit it in!) but we think it would have pleased her greatly that for many years now members have contested for a trophy for the game, presented annually at the Conference.

And so there we have the picture, regrettably somewhat sketchy, of our first ever Secretary of Inner Wheel in Great Britain and Ireland; a quiet, unassuming personality; a kindly, diplomatic pourer of oil on troubled waters; possessed of a dry wit; a tireless worker behind the scenes — an example to all who assume the duties of Secretary at any level in the organisation. In 1955 Gladys Mabel Nixon died at the relatively early age of sixty-seven.

Mrs. Gladys Young

Talking to Mrs. Gladys Young is a stimulating experience. Blessed with total recall she racily takes one back in time to the early days in Inner Wheel just as if it all happened yesterday.

Originally Gladys was a Lancashire lass, born and bred in Blackpool. Her Inner Wheel life though began in Canterbury. She was a Founder Member of the Canterbury Ladies' 'Wheel of Service' before it changed its name to Inner Wheel. She is still a member of the Canterbury Club in No. 12 District and has been both President and Treasurer of it. For her District she has acted as Secretary, Treasurer and Council Member. Founder Treasurer of the Association, she held that office for ten years. Undoubtedly though she is remembered most of all for the years she served as Secretary/Treasurer for the Association. Incredible as it seems today she undertook that combined office in 1939, taking up the Secretaryship where Mrs. Nixon left off. Until 1945 she carried out this dual role and even when a Treasurer, Mrs. R. H. Tomalin (G. V. Toomey) was appointed, still continued as Association Secretary for a further four years. Immediately after World War II there was a tremendous upsurge of extension. Two hundred and ninety-nine new Clubs formed within Great Britain and Ireland; twenty-three new Clubs Overseas; and four new Districts, and yet, in conversation, Gladys Young lightly dismisses what must have been an alarming, ever-mounting mass of paper-work for her, by saying: 'Oh, I managed all right working from home.'

Gladys is the widow of J. H. B. Young, D.S.O., M.C., J.P., by profession a chartered accountant who held many offices in Rotary, becoming R.I.B.I. President in 1946 and later a Director of Rotary International. He not only greatly encouraged Gladys in her work for Inner Wheel but lent her much practical aid. He it was who took the Minutes of the meeting in Douglas, Isle of Man, when the Association formed. He it was who acted as Auditor for the Association for a time, giving of his professional expertise and office facilities to produce the Association's Annual Balance Sheets. Nor did the contribution made by the Young family stop there. Gladys's only daughter, Dorothea, now headmistress of a school in Canterbury, played a part, for it was she who with great skill and artistry lettered the Charters granted to the early Clubs. She was, incidentally, paid the princely sum of three shillings and sixpence for each!

Without any doubt then Gladys Young was one of the chief builders of the Association for it was she who coped throughout the war years when administration was at its most difficult and the organisation could so easily have floundered. Some measure of her wisdom and foresight comes through to us in a speech she delivered all those years ago, firstly on a subject she felt strongly about. 'I would like to see a resolution passed,' she said, 'that the Constitution remain unaltered for three years. Then there might be a chance of some of us really learning it!'. And secondly, from the same address came the stern advice: 'Our thoughts and energies should be directed towards the vital problems of our day. To do this we need good leadership and for this careful selection of Club Delegates. Don't choose Mrs. X because it is "her turn" if she is not fitted for the job, but rather Mrs. Y because she has real ability, even if she is a more recently joined member.'

Gladys Young does not spare herself today any more than she once did in maintaining standards for Inner Wheel. She is just as deeply concerned as she was in her youth. A few tangible tributes have been paid to her as time has passed; a silver salver on her twenty-fifth wedding anniversary in 1946; a silver spoon engraved with the Inner Wheel emblem in 1974 when she handed over to the Association for their records all her own personal working papers of the original constitutional minutes; but perhaps the most treasured gift she ever received was the lovely pearl necklace and ear-rings she still wears with pride and affection. The presentation was made to her at the 1949 Conference by Association President, Jessie Park, all members having contributed. Wittily Mrs. Park in her address referred to Mrs. Young's birthplace, Blackpool, and her present place of residence, Whitstable. Gladys, she said, might be likened to a stick of Blackpool rock but it would be 'Inner Wheel' which would be stamped right through, or better perhaps to liken her to a Whitstable oyster where, in one in a long while, was discovered a pearl of great price. And so Gladys Young demitted the office of Association Secretary after so many years of hard work. Nothing can ever repay her — except perhaps our continued and devoted friendship.

When asked ten years later to recall her feelings when she gave up office, succinctly Gladys wrote a summary of her emotions in the Association Magazine — 'Thrill at the recollection of the meeting in Douglas when the Association formed. Amazement when appointed Honorary Treasurer at the first meeting of Council a few weeks later (Dues were then sixpence a member!). Amazement at the Presidential hats of great variety at our Conferences. Pleasure through the years I was privileged to work with Mabel Nixon to whom the Association owes more than can ever be said. Anxiety in 1939 when I was appointed Secretary/Treasurer and many Clubs in coastal towns had to close down. Relief in 1941 when progress was resumed. Excitement in 1945 when R.I.B.I. President T. H. Rose came to a Council meeting to express Rotarian thanks for the help given to Rotary during the war. Contentment when in 1948 the Association had grown to the status requiring its own headquarters and a whole time Secretary, with five hundred Clubs in these islands and thirty-five overseas. Thankfulness for the wonderful friendship given to me.'

That says it all and illustrates far better than any words of ours could, the vibrant, effervescent personality that is — Mrs. Gladys Young.

Mrs. Millicent Gaskell

Few of us read a book, without at some point speculating about the author of it, and many members who have not met Mrs. Millicent Gaskell must be curious about her. History requires to be written periodically in the interests of successive generations and so it is fitting to record here and try to acknowledge sincerely and gratefully the enormous, indeed quite incalculable service done for Inner Wheel by the writer of the only history of it ever written to date — 'HOME AND HORIZON', the work of Mrs. Millicent Gaskell, now a member of the Colne Club, No. 19 District. With this book, first published in 1953 and later reprinted in 1964 every member must be by now familiar and fond. The very title is inspired for it is both neat and apt and throughout the years in its pages every one of us at some time must have sought and found information, guidance and much wisdom.

Born in 1905 and educated at Bacup and Rawtenstall Grammar School, Mrs. Gaskell graduated at Manchester University with First Class Honours in English and a Diploma in Education and taught until she married Rotarian Eric J. Gaskell. She has a daughter and two sons and is happily blest with nine grandchildren.

Mrs. Gaskell is not a contemporary of our Founder for she joined Inner Wheel in 1939, a few months after Mrs. Golding's death. To call her 'a dedicated member' may seem trite, but a more appropriate description of her would be hard to find, for she has not, by any means, confined her service to the Association to the written record of its history. The list of offices she has held makes lesser mortals look upon her with awe. Like the present writer (but only in that one respect!) she has been a member of three Clubs. She has been Correspondent for, and President of all three, indeed has been President twice for one of them. Moreover she has served as a Club Secretary and has held the office of District Editor. The last District Chairman of No. 5 District before it divided for the second time, she became the Founder Chairman of No. 19 District and finally in 1949 was elected President of the Association.

It was a challenging and eventful year in which to take on the duties of President, so many innovations were taking place. The Association was renting for the first time premises in London from which to operate, the first paid Secretary was newly appointed and it was now that R.I.B.I. put to Inner Wheel that it should hold its first independent Conference. All these circumstances presented new situations, new problems, but heroically Millicent Gaskell coped, and when her Presidential year was over, reviewing it with her customary meticulous attention to detail, she recorded that she had received some seven hundred and thirty-four letters; eighteen postcards; one hundred and sixty-five Minutes and Reports; two hundred and eighty-eight Bulletins and fifty-one Notices, every word of which she had read with interest and nearly all with pleasure. In reply she had sent out eight hundred and twenty-two letters and four hundred and sixteen postcards. She had travelled around thirteen thousand, five hundred and seventy-one miles; addressed an aggregate of over six thousand members on her District visits and had spoken to two thousand, two hundred members at the Harrogate Conference. Moreover, towards the end of her year as President she had gone to France, there to present the Charter to the Inner Wheel Club of Valenciennes, the first French Club to form.

One would be forgiven for thinking that surely all of that

31

would amount to an admirable sum total of one woman's endeavour within the framework of one of her interests, for she had and has many more, but not a bit of it! When in 1952 it was deemed necessary to set up an Ad Hoc Committee on Constitution for Overseas Districts it was she who was its Chairman and again later she became Chairman of the Ad Hoc Committee on Constitution for International Inner Wheel.

In pursuit of information among the archives of the Association, articles and copious notes surface; copies of speeches and reports given are discovered, and when one seeks the writer's name, yes, it transpires they are all the work of — who else, but Millicent Gaskell. Knowledgeable, indefatigable and yes, it has to be repeated 'dedicated' as she is, it comes then as no surprise to anyone that, holding a record of service to Rotary as great as hers to Inner Wheel, is her husband, R.I.B.I. Past President, Eric J. Gaskell.

Justice of the Peace, Educationalist, Soroptimist, Author and Historian — it is no fulsome tribute but a richly deserved one to observe that Millicent Gaskell is truly a woman of many gifts, skills and much industry and has played and is still playing a very active and constructive part in the development of Inner Wheel.

Many, many more are those deserving of mention. Limited, alas, the space here in which to do them justice, but nothing and no one is lost sight of as the years go by. Records of all who in any way have contributed right from the beginning, their names, what they did and when are kept with care at Headquarters. It makes an impressive catalogue of personal achievements. Thomas Carlyle was indeed correct. History is the essence of innumerable biographies.

Going Nationwide

INNER WHEEL, like Rotary, is concerned primarily with the giving of service to community needs within the immediate environs of its many Clubs. It is true both organisations have grown to the extent of world-wide caring, but equally true, and only natural that, for the individual member, home wherever it is for them, is nearest to their hearts, and so all are wont in a work like this to turn to where they are mentioned.

It has been told how it was in the north-west of England Inner Wheel was born, the Manchester Club referred to by most as 'Mother of them All' and how the first ever District was formed in that area. No. 5 District was to extend vigorously in all directions. It was to divide twice, creating out of itself No. 18 District in 1936 and No. 19 District in 1947, but even so it still remains one of the largest Districts and retains eight of the '79 ers'. It has also continued to make valuable contribution to Inner Wheel growth by supplying the Association with several distinguished Presidents and Officers.

Now let us examine very briefly how Inner Wheel grew up in other regions and countries within Great Britain and Ireland and go NATIONWIDE . . .

The giving of the following short District summaries, it must be emphasised, does not indicate comparison in any way. Competition between Clubs and Districts has always been thoroughly discouraged. On many things depends the rate of growth in any one area, density of population the obvious one. All Districts have contributed equally. Without any one of them the Association would be the poorer.

It is a fascinating study to dig down to the very grass roots where possible. When, for instance, in 1936, Mrs. E. Gower (Putney), then Chairman of No. 13 District, on the day Mrs. Golding made Charter Presentations to twelve Clubs in the

Rembrandt Hotel, Kensington, remarked: 'We will be making history today,' she spoke more prophetically than she knew. Admittedly in such a populous area as embraced by No. 13 District (London and its immediate environs) the growth potential was unequalled in the country but that must not blind us to the magnitude of the early effort made there for extension of the movement.

The District had formed in 1932 at Carpenter's Restaurant, Clapham, with Mrs. Golding addressing members from the five Founder Clubs of Clapham (1926); Kensington (1927); Brixton (1929); Hackney (1930); and Putney (1932). Subsequently the District Committee came into being at the home of Mrs. W. A. Shakerley (Clapham) who was later to succeed Mrs. Golding as Association President. By the end of 1936 there were sixteen Clubs and by 1939 there were twenty-two of them and heroically four more formed during the war. The big breakthrough arrived though with the cessation of hostilities and the forming of an Extension Committee under the leadership of Mrs. R. Gordon Bradley (Putney). Then a truly sensational development (such as never had been known before or likely ever to be again) took place. Forty-one Clubs established within five years. Little wonder that to mark such a spectacular achievement, a triumphant District Luncheon was held in 1951 in honour of Mrs. Gordon Bradley's work. The venue was the Holburn Hotel and the Association President of the time, Mrs. T. H. Gameson, presented to Mrs. Gordon Bradley a bound, illuminated Address, in it the treasured signatures of a whole District.

Interviewed many years later, Mrs. Gordon Bradley said modestly: 'I would hate to sound egotistical. I was just fortunate that Extension work came my way after the static years of war.' *Fortunate* is not the word we would use of such results. Maybe the time *was* ripe but the endeavour must have been monumental. What is more, Mrs. Gordon Bradley had not confined her promotion of Inner Wheel to her own No. 13 District but had been instrumental in forming Clubs overseas, that of Port Elizabeth, South Africa, in 1938, and much later in 1946, the Club of Singapore.

Once so strongly established No. 13 District never looked

back. In 1964 there were seventy-five Clubs with a total membership of over two thousand. True a few Clubs have disbanded in the area but this has not appreciably diminished the undoubted strength of the District, although it was especially sad to lose as recently as in 1975 the Club of Brixton which started life as the 'Ladies' Guild of Service' as long ago as in 1929 and had given so much service undeterred even by the complete destruction of all their records by a bomb which fell on the Brixton Astoria, their meeting place. There remain, however, six '79 ers' in the District and from here in the early days and much more recently too have come members to serve at Association level.

Strong bonds of affection and understanding have always existed between No. 13 District and its nearest neighbours, No. 12 District and No. 14 District. Formed in the same year, they grew up together. All three are geographically admirably suited for overseas contact and they have countless visitors from the Continent at Club and District meetings.

Like No. 13 District, No. 14 District came into being with five Clubs; those of Brighton (1932); Guildford (1926); Littlehampton (1926); Teddington (1928); and Wimbledon (1930) and although there are much older Clubs here — to be exact, nine are '79 ers' — among other distinctions of this District is that it has the first Inner Wheel Club to be formed after the outbreak of war, that of Carshalton. In 1940 this Club received its Charter from Association President, Mrs. L. W. Barnard, and despite its extremely vulnerable geographical position it never once missed holding a monthly meeting during all the years of enemy air activity. It made indeed the welfare of the local searchlight unit its special care.

Although acknowledging the work of Association President, Mrs. Jessie Park, of No. 3 District as the first of its kind in the field of starting holiday schemes for people in dire need of rest and care, members in No. 14 District have cause to take pride in the splendid effort made by their member, Mary Preston (Surbiton) who when District Chairman in 1953, impressed by Mrs. Park's idea, began a similar scheme which was, at the time, intended to last for only one year, but was so successful that it is still flourishing today.

From No. 14 District have come several Association Presidents and Officers, prominent among them Mrs. W. E. Coote (Wimbledon) in 1946. Mrs. Coote was Founder Chairman of the District and it was she who first envisaged a history of Inner Wheel being written. Assiduously she set about collecting material, spending three years after her Presidential one on the work, and managing to record true histories of the first four hundred Clubs. Much of her writing survives today. Mrs. Millicent Gaskell graciously dedicated 'HOME AND HORIZON' to her and the present writer has been glad to turn time and time again to her notes. The District has further cause for pride for it was Mrs. D. M. Weightman (Purley) who was elected in 1967 to the office of first President of International Inner Wheel.

No. 12 District has the honour to have of its number eleven '79 ers'. It formed in 1932 with representatives from the Clubs of Bexhill (1924); Chatham (1929); Folkestone (1932); Gillingham (1930), and Canterbury (1925) with Ashford's 'Rotary Ladies' attending.

The District has grown steadily. In 1972 there were all of forty-seven Clubs with a membership of nearly one thousand, five hundred, and in that year to commemorate forty years of friendship and working together members held a service of thanksgiving in Canterbury Cathedral.

Conditions during the war years, as can be understood, were difficult for this District due to its geographical position, but as frequently is the case, a personality emerged equal to the challenge. From 1943 until 1945 Mrs. E. Lumley-Robinson (Gillingham) was the District's Chairman and she will always be remembered for the way in which, often ignoring personal travel hazards, she went about stimulating and extending interest in the organisation. Now in 1976 a nonagenarian, Mrs. Lumley-Robinson is still an active, interested member. Associated with No. 12 District in the minds of members everywhere is, and always will be, of course, the name and work of Mrs. Gladys Young (Canterbury), but from here too came Mrs. E. M. Billingham (Ramsgate) to be Association President *and* the first Auditor for the Association; Mrs. L. Lack (Dartford) to be first Secretary of International Inner

Wheel and Mrs. G. Sarjeant to be Editor of the International Inner Wheel Magazine.

Of the same vintage year as Districts No. 12, 13 and 14, was No. 10 District, although since 1972 it has been divided into No. 10 and No. 20 Districts. The Founder Clubs of No. 10 District were four in number. Those of Bristol (1924); Cheltenham (1931); Gloucester (1931) and Weston-super-Mare (1932). Prior to becoming an Inner Wheel Club, wives of Bristol Rotarians had been known as the 'Ladies' Auxiliary' with an extremely impressive record of community service.

Live memories of such old Clubs as these and the actual forming of them are today naturally somewhat scarce and therefore greatly to be prized. One such comes our way from Mrs. O. Mountain Palmer, a Founder member of the Cheltenham Club, now in her eighty-ninth year and presently a member of the Ruislip-Northwood Club in District No. 9. It is a remarkably clear, racy account of how she remembers several Rotary wives meeting at a small restaurant in Cheltenham High Street in 1930 to consider the idea of Inner Wheel and of how they decided then to make a start, and were eventually in 1937 honoured by a visit from Mrs. Golding, who gave them her blessing. 'There was no such thing as social security in those days and the Club's activities consisted of sending delicate girls to a convalescent home in Weston-super-Mare which meant finding suitable clothing to send them in!' Mrs. Mountain Palmer writes. She remembers well the day she became Club Secretary to Mrs. L. W. Barnard (later in 1939 to become Association President) and tells of another day during the war when as a member of the St. John Ambulance Brigade she got back home after hospital duty at the Army hospital on the Cheltenham Race Course to find a telephone message from the President. Would she take the Inner Wheel meeting? The President's daughter was ill. 'Owing to the blackout,' she recounts, 'we had to meet very early in the afternoon. Swallowing a hasty lunch and still in uniform I rushed to the meeting just in time to greet the speaker, and sat there with my respirator and tin helmet under my chair and my bicycle at the ready outside for I was also a member of the Mobile First Aid Unit.' Such stuff as early No. 10 District members were made of! Mrs. Mountain Palmer signs herself — 'An Old Campaigner'. She was indeed.

Division has not weakened No. 10 District. It forges ahead, can look back with justifiable pride on its past achievements and it cherishes the four '79 ers' which are still within its boundaries.

In the following year of 1933 Inner Wheel was to get a hold in the North, for both No. 3 and No. 4 Districts formed.

No. 3 District extends from Darlington in the South to Berwick-on-Tweed in the North and its three Founder Clubs were those of Sunderland (1929); Whitley Bay (1930); and Gateshead (1932) all three with long and noble records of early service. Certainly causes deserving of their help were not difficult for these young Clubs to find at the time. The Gateshead Club, for example, was set up when something like 49% of the population in the town were without work. The situation was a challenge, the spirit among Club members equal to it and much wonderful work was done to alleviate distress in the worst hit areas. Today Gateshead boasts two Clubs, the original one and that of Gateshead East (1958).

The inaugural meeting of this District was held in Tilley's Cafe, Newcastle-on-Tyne and at it one member from Sunderland and one from Whitley Bay was elected to attend the meeting of the Central Organisation Interim Committee in London to draft the Constitution and By-Laws. Mrs. Golding came in person to Gateshead in the spring of 1938 and there addressed an Inter-Club meeting.

From among the District's many well-known members one is especially beloved and remembered — Mrs. Jessie Park (South Shields) who made an immense, enthusiastic contribution to the movement. Long before she became President of the Association in 1948 she gave valuable assistance in the setting up of the first District in Scotland. In 1946, on becoming first Chairman of the then International Committee which office was coupled with that of Overseas Correspondent, with great effect she encouraged Clubs to appoint members to contact Clubs overseas and many lasting friendships resulted and within her own District she greatly endeared herself. Together with her husband, Rotarian Norman Park, between the years 1948/1966 she worked ceaselessly on a project to provide holidays for needy people, arranging for them to be housed and looked after in Alnmouth and Marske, and this eventually became a corporate effort in No. 3 District.

The three Founder Clubs are naturally '79 ers', but the District has every cause to take pride in its more recent contributions too, for from it has come members to hold the office of Association President, one who was also Association Treasurer, and a member who, after being Editor of the Magazine in Great Britain and Ireland, went on to become Editor of the International Magazine.

One of the largest northern Districts at the present moment, with over sixty Clubs and a long history of service, is No. 4 District. Its origins go back to the forming of three Clubs all within eighteen miles of each other in South Yorkshire — Doncaster (1928); Sheffield (1931) and Rotherham (1933), the last named unfortunately no longer with us since 1973 after all of forty years' consistent, loyal service, the only casualty in the District.

It seems several discussions took place between these three Clubs before they finally came to the decision to form a District with a Sheffield member as its Chairman, but once started extension in the area was rapid. There were eleven Clubs in existence by the time Mrs. Golding and Mrs. Nixon came to the first No. 4 District Rally in June 1936, and all received their Charters that day. (Sheffield's Charter today is a replica, the original having been destroyed in an air raid in 1940.)

From the outset the District appears to have been full of enthusiasm and ideas. It is on record that as early as in 1932 the Doncaster Club actually put forward the suggestion that Inner Wheel should have its own *monthly* Magazine, and although this was never to be, it is very evident still that this area has a distinct leaning towards written communication as a means of promoting endeavour, for a great many of their Club Bulletins today contain bracing, philosophical observations calculated to make their members sit up and take notice. That this is effectual is demonstrated by the remarkable response which is made in service. With true Yorkshire industry Clubs support with fervour every known cause. You name it, in fact, and No. 4 District has contributed to it.

Of the District's '79 ers' eight remain and the District has played its part nobly in providing the Association with several of its Presidents and Officers.

In the same year as those two northern Districts formed one further south was founded, No. 8 District, its Founder Clubs those of Colchester, which as far back as in 1927 was operating under the name of the 'Women's Auxiliary'; Norwich (1928); Grays Thurrock (1932) and Chelmsford (1933).

In this case District formation was directly attributable to a chance visit paid by two members of the Grays Thurrock Club to a No. 13 District meeting in 1933. On their return the members concerned forthwith arranged a combined meeting of the four Clubs in their area. As a result the District formed, Colchester supplying the Founder Chairman, Chelmsford the Vice-Chairman and Grays Thurrock the Secretary/Treasurer. Extension at once began with a Club forming at Great Yarmouth in the following year. Clubs formed at King's Lynn and Ipswich in 1937; in Felixstowe and Cambridge in 1939 and in Lowestoft in 1940, and it is interesting to note that all early District Meetings were arranged to coincide with Rotary ones 'to save on transport' as this was then a relatively sparsely populated and scattered area.

During the war years extension slowed but the existing Clubs all entered with great verve into supporting Association corporate efforts making substantial contributions. Immediately the emergency was over extension picked up rapidly. In 1974 there was a total of fifty-eight Clubs in the region. Then came division with the southern portion of the District becoming the new No. 24 District. For such an old District this parting of the ways inevitably brought with it a sense of loss, particularly as henceforth No. 8 District was to have within its boundaries far fewer Clubs. It did, in fact, lose three of the ones which founded it, and only the Clubs of Norwich and Great Yarmouth are the '79 ers' left to it. Happily, however, extension proceeds and very deeply felt bonds of affection exist between the 'young' and the 'old' District. Friendships are kept alive, joint luncheons between past and present members of the Executive Committees of both Districts are held and District No. 8 continues to give service to the Association worthy of its beginnings.

District No. 6 was the only one to form in the year 1934, and the story of its foundation must always be associated with the Club of Wolverhampton which formed in 1930 with a membership of around thirty and functioned and flourished alone for three years, until due to the efforts of its members and the work of its Founder President, Lady Mander, in particular, plus a visit from Mrs. Golding, the Clubs of Worcester (1933) and West Bromwich (1934) joined it.

With these three Clubs the District established. In quick succession three more formed; that of North Staffs. (now known as Stoke-on-Trent); the Walsall Club; and that of Stourbridge, this last Club now disbanded after forty years' devoted service. The formation of the Nuneaton Club and Coventry Club followed in 1935, making in all eight by 1936. Today there are over thirty Clubs. At one time Clubs totalled seventy-five but divisional changes drastically reduced that number, indeed divorced the three Founder Clubs from each other. West Bromwich alone remaining within the District.

To date the District has gallantly provided the Association with four Presidents, the first of them Mrs. H. Barnacle (Coventry) who to commemorate her year in office conceived the idea of presenting to her District what is now known as the Barnacle Trophy. It takes the form of a silver rose-bowl and initially was given to Clubs with the highest annual membership attendance. Over the years, however, the attendance percentage in the older Clubs fell as it is wont to do and now the Barnacle Trophy is held annually by the Club of the District Chairman.

No. 11 District, formed in 1936, is an interesting one and certainly unique in one respect, that two of its Founder Clubs, Shanklin and Sandown, both formed in 1934, were not even on the mainland but on the Isle of Wight. They were joined in 1935 by the Club of Salisbury and that of Portsmouth and Southsea in 1936 and towards the end of that year the first District meeting took place in Kimble's Cafe, Southsea.

From records of the proceedings of that first District

meeting it is evident members got down to serious work without delay. From it they put several proposals to the Association Council, one in particular which they were to press for many times — that Inner Wheel should have a separate journal, or at least a folder for its news, rather than rely upon the generosity of Rotary for a page in its Magazine.

Within the District's inaugural year a second District meeting was held in Shanklin and a third at Sandown and already by then the membership in Portsmouth and Southsea had risen to over fifty. Today it has an even larger membership. With the formation of a committee for extension work Clubs grew steadily in number. Now there are forty of them, remarkably seven where it all began — on the Isle of Wight itself. Two more island Clubs flourish now in this District; Jersey (1946) and Guernsey (1947) from which members travel enthusiastically to attend all District meetings.

The original two Clubs are, of course, '79 ers' and many are the members who have come forward to serve the Association down the years, from as far back as in 1944 when Mrs. R. H. Tomalin (G. V. Toomey) of the Salisbury Club then, but now of the Bristol Club in No. 10 District, was elected to the office of Association Treasurer.

Another District which was to form in 1936 was No. 17 which lies in the picturesque extreme south west. It started life in Goodbody's Cafe, Bedford Street, Plymouth, which town was selected as most convenient because of its central position. Five Clubs were involved; that of Exmouth which had been in existence since 1930 and very much out on its own in the south; Torquay (1934); and Falmouth, Penzance and Bideford, all in 1936.

Each of those five Clubs contributed to the formation of the first District Committee. The Torquay Club's formation was first discussed by Rotary wives in the canteen kitchen of a Social Centre for the unemployed set up by Rotary. Mrs. P. Almy became the Club's first President and later the District's Founder Chairman. Exmouth provided the District Secretary; Falmouth (the first Inner Wheel Club in Cornwall) the Vice-President; Penzance the Treasurer and Bideford two delegates.

Both Exmouth and Torquay are '79 ers' and proud of it. The Bideford Club was forced to disband for a while but happily returned to the fold in 1962. Throughout the years of war the District battled on, one District Chairman and her Secretary are indeed remembered as having resorted to touring the District on bicycles rather than let interest in the movement wane and the District even grew in that time for both the Truro and Paignton Clubs formed in 1944. Post-war extension was considerable. Today there are over forty Clubs, including one out on the lovely Isles of Scilly, founded in 1972 and from which come members by sea or plane to be present at District meetings.

Elected to the office of Association Treasurer have been two members from the District, one of whom subsequently became President of the Association in 1973.

Partly in England, partly in Wales No. 18 District was the only other District to form in 1936. Today well-established, it is active and ever-growing. Geographically it embraces both great cities and small townships; Liverpool, the largest and oldest of its Clubs, membership presently in the eighties; Holyhead, the smallest, membership around a dozen. Industrial Merseyside, picturesque Pwllheli, historic Chester, celebrated Caernarvon, all lie within its boundaries. At the moment there are thirty-nine Clubs, twenty-three of them, we are informed, strictly speaking in North Wales, but the city of Liverpool is where it all began, way back before many present members were born, in 1916, to be exact, and it started by, of all things, an auction sale of 'White Elephants' at the Rushworth Hall.

The Rotary Club of Liverpool was holding this in aid of the Lord Mayor's Fund for widows and dependants of the fallen and disabled of the First World War. Naturally for such an event they enlisted the help of their wives in collecting, cleaning and sorting of the items for sale. After it was all over the ladies involved felt strongly that they wanted to retain the friendships they had made in the process. The title of the

Club they formed was firstly, simply 'Rotary Ladies'. Later they called themselves 'The Service Club'. In 1918 Liverpool Rotarians opened an Information kiosk to assist members of H.M. Forces passing through their city. Here again the wives gave help, staffing the kiosk during the day, the Rotarians taking over by night.

With the war over 'The Service Club' undertook many community services but it was discovered that the name 'Service Club' was being confused with another organisation in the city, and as it so happened, it was about this time that Mrs. Golding was appealing to all Rotary wives who had formed Clubs of any sort to adopt the name of 'Inner Wheel'. She visited the 'Service Club' once or twice and suggested to the ladies that they might like to come under the umbrella of the name 'Inner Wheel'. It is recorded, however, that for a while they were reluctant but eventually concurred. This time-lag eliminates any foundation — even if there was no other — for the claim that Liverpool was the first Club. It may very well have been the first Club of Rotary wives to form — that we fear can never now be firmly established. It may even be that the Rules we work to today were Rules first thought of by those Rotary wives in Liverpool, but the first Club of Rotary wives to be known as an Inner Wheel one was indisputably that of Manchester. In any event, both Clubs celebrated their 50th Anniversary in the same month in the same year — October 1973.

It is unfortunate that enemy action robbed us of ever reading the Liverpool Club's first records. What we do have, however, are precious personal written recollections of the formation of No. 18 District and of the major part the Liverpool Club played in it, for it supplied both its Founder Chairman and Secretary.

When the Rotary Clubs of Merseyside and North Wales were taken from the No. 5 Rotary District to form their No. 18 District there were only three Inner Wheel Clubs left in the new area, Liverpool, Bangor (both 79 ers) and Prestatyn (1935) and for a while they remained in No. 5 District. On the formation of the Club of Wrexham, however, it was decided a No. 18 District could form. Accordingly at the Blossoms

Hotel, Chester, with Mrs. Golding and Mrs. Nixon both present, the inaugural meeting was held.

Bumper years for extension here were those between 1944 and 1950 in which time fourteen new Clubs came into being and that year brought further development in that the District held its first Assembly of Club Officers and the first edition of the District's Bulletin appeared, and at time of writing No. 18 District has presented the Association with members who have nobly held high office, one Association Editor who was also Vice-President, one Association Treasurer and two Association Presidents.

Tracing the beginning of No. 7 District to its source leads us back in time to the forming of the Kettering Club in the autumn of 1935. The Club received its Charter from Mrs. Golding who, accompanied by Mrs. Nixon, stopped off on a journey back to Manchester one day and called in at one of the Club's fortnightly meetings. Founder members well remember the address she gave and how inspiring they found it. The Kettering Club was destined, however, to work entirely out on its own for all of three years, then quite quickly was joined by three others: Loughborough; Northampton; and Grimsby and Cleethorpes, and so the District formed at the end of 1938 with Mrs. Gower, the Association President of the time, presiding at the inaugural meeting.

In 1939 the first District meeting was held and one more Club was founded in Nottingham. Peterborough then formed in 1940. Then, as in all other areas, extension marked time. The District's first Rally was, however, held in 1941 at Lincoln. In 1946 the first No. 7 District Magazine made its appearance and in 1951 the District gave the Association an Editor who held office for five years and later became Association President and again in 1961 another Association President was to come from this area.

The District has survived well the division of it in 1972 into No. 7 and No. 22 Districts and of recent date extension has begun again.

Hotel, Chester, with Mrs. Golding and Mrs. Nixon both present, the inaugural meeting was held.

Bumper years for excursions here were those between 1944 and 1950 and that was reflected in No. 18's coming into being hold as it was in the proud context of the District the District Association with its meetings held. No. 18 District Association with members who have hobly held high office one Association Editor who was

'We'll keep a welcome in the hillsides,
We'll keep a welcome in the vales,
This land you knew will still be singing
When you come home again to Wales.'
ORIGINAL WELSH LYRIC.

Development of Inner Wheel was bound to flourish in Wales, not because it was the brain-child of a woman of Welsh extraction particularly, but rather because of the very nature of the people whether they live in the north or the southern part of it. 'Wild Wales' may be an apt geographical description, but members who hail from there merit other epithets. Sensitive, kindly and overwhelmingly hospitable it was to be expected they would take to their hearts the purposes of the movement and they have done just that, giving unstintingly of their services when local disasters (of which unfortunately they have had their share) have struck, and embracing too all causes both national and international.

From the District map we see how in the south of Wales lies No. 15 District, marginally within its boundaries the town of Hay-on-Wye, birthplace of Mrs. Golding. It is though, to the town of Newport we must look to find the District's Mother Club. There in 1930 several Rotary wives met at Cefn Mably Hospital to mend linen. In as humble a service as that lie our Welsh beginnings. Later they started to meet in the Mount Pleasant Hospital where their husbands already were regular visitors. In this hospital they began to teach veterans from the First World War to embroider and participate in other crafts and from engaging together in this way, among the thirty-four women concerned arose the idea of forming a Rotary Ladies' Guild. Unfortunately this Guild did not keep records of their activities except on the financial side. In the Treasurer's book under January 20th, 1931 there appears the small item of eleven shillings and two pence for travelling expenses paid to a certain Mrs. Golding — first evidence of the move towards setting up an Inner Wheel Club in the area.

There is later mention of the bank account being transferred to one for Inner Wheel and in 1934 the Club of Newport finally chartered, thus qualifying to be a '79 er', the only one in No. 15 District.

By 1938 there were seven Clubs; those of Newport itself; Cardiff; Pontypool; Aberdare; Barry; Swansea and Llandrindod Wells and at a gathering of them all the District formed, the oldest Club of Newport supplying the Chairman; Cardiff providing the Vice-Chairman and Pontypool the Secretary/Treasurer. The first of the District's meetings was held in Swansea where Club Charters were presented; it was decreed that future District meetings should coincide in date with Rotary District ones; present were interested observers from both Abertillery and Haverfordwest and it was announced that a Club had formed at Carmarthen.

By 1939 there were ten Clubs in existence and their record of war service is second to none. Immediately on the outbreak of hostilities members were adjured to welcome into their Clubs any members evacuated from danger zones. Every single Club engaged immediately to aid those on active service, and in passing it is interesting to note the unusual avenues of service they found. The Barry Club, for example, undertook to supply fresh vegetables to the lightship stationed in the Bristol Channel whilst the Club of Swansea provided all manner of comforts for the twelve mine-sweepers adopted by the Rotary Club there. Other Districts were, of course, doing equally fine war work but perhaps did not have quite the same physical problems with which to contend, for it is still remembered how on two occasions during the war years No. 15 District had to postpone District Meetings due to arctic weather ('Wild Wales', remember?), but they soldiered on regardless.

Extension since has been vigorous and today there are over thirty Clubs, including the thousandth one to be formed in Great Britain and Ireland, that of Llantrisant (1976) and there have been no disbandments, although the Clubs of Chepstow and Monmouth have been transferred now to No. 10 District. The District produced its first Bulletin in 1946, a quarterly, now known as 'The Spokeswoman', following the Rotary

47

publication for the area which is known as 'The *Spokes*man', illustrative of Welsh wit.

As the years have passed many No. 15 District members have held positions of importance for the Association and in the spring of 1974 to celebrate the Golden Jubilee of the founding of Inner Wheel Clubs members from all over the District met together for a service of thanksgiving and re-dedication in Brecon Cathedral.

Especially for the occasion a choir of members had been trained under the direction of the then District Chairman, and those present tell of how moved and inspired they were by the beauty of those Welsh voices and appropriately the lesson was read by the only Association President, to date, to come from No. 15 District, Mrs. D. M. Parry (Pontypridd).

Congratulations, Wales! Llongyfarchiadau, Cymru!

When a number of Rotary wives accompanied their husbands to the 1937 R.I.B.I. Conference in Bournemouth little did they dream that before the week-end was over they would have decided to form the Inner Wheel Club of Uxbridge, which in turn was to become the Mother Club of No. 9 District, but such was the case.

The ladies had been invited to the Annual General Meeting of the Association. There they met Mrs. Golding and saw the Presidential ring presented to her. Need we say more? They returned home impressed. The President of the Rotary Club of Uxbridge then kindly extended an invitation to his home to all Uxbridge Rotary wives and forthwith the Uxbridge Inner Wheel Club was born, its first President, his wife — and here we cannot resist the temptation to digress momentarily to record evidence of how friendship within Inner Wheel can lead to romance (and no doubt there are innumerable other instances!). Mrs. Wade, President of the new Club, naturally enough wished for guidance in her role. No. 13 District had taken the Uxbridge Club under its wing and in Mrs. Gordon Bradley from that District Mrs. Wade found a good and helpful friend. In the course of time Mrs. Bradley's daughter met

Mrs. Wade's nephew and when they married Mrs. Gordon Bradley's daughter immediately became an enthusiastic member of the Uxbridge Club.

In those days Charter Presentations were simple affairs. (Might we be well-advised to revert in these days of austerity?) The Uxbridge Club received its Charter from the No. 13 District Chairman in the Great Central Hotel, Marylebone. The Club worked extremely hard and by 1939 had persuaded Rotary wives to form the Club of Windsor and Eton. In 1944 the two Clubs of Watford and Rickmansworth formed and so there were four . . . Time for a District to be inaugurated, but even before the date was settled upon, Clubs in Hertford and St. Albans had come into being, and High Wycombe followed in 1945.

Now, unlike most other Districts which appear to have got off to a good start on sunny days with no snags arising, No. 9 District had problems. The obvious venue for the inauguration ceremony was Uxbridge itself, but Uxbridge had suffered badly in the bombing. Everything was looking shabby and run-down. There simply was no suitable meeting place. Finally a gallant Rotarian saved the situation by offering the use of a lecture hall in the Education Buildings. A simple afternoon meeting it was to be, with a wartime tea in a nearby cinema cafe afterwards. The day arrived. The rain poured down. Members arrived after dismal journeys, not in the best of moods, to be informed that, due to illness, the Association President could not personally attend.

So accompanied by the Association Secretary, the Association Vice-President came to deputise, and kindly and thoughtfully, but unexpectedly, an Association *Past* President came too, but only *two* bouquets were at the ready! How to split them into three? It is not disclosed how the emergency was resolved and is an amusing subject for speculation. Despite this less than propitious start, however, all was carried through. District Offices were filled by an equal number of Uxbridge and Windsor members and District No. 9 was born.

From then on it never faltered. By 1950 there were over twenty Clubs and today the number has much more than doubled and to No. 9 District the Association is indebted

c

greatly, for from it has come one member to be Association Editor, one to be Association Treasurer and two Presidents.

> 'They say there's bread and work for all
> And the sun shines always there.
> But I'll not forget old Ireland
> Were it fifty times as fair.'
>
> HELEN BLACKWOOD, LADY DUFFERIN.

Rotary came to Europe via Ireland for the first ever Rotary Club in Europe was established in Dublin in the spring of 1911 (and now there are three in that city), and only a few months later in the same year the first Belfast Rotary Club formed (and now there are three of them in that city too). All of twenty years were to pass, however, before the first Inner Wheel Club in Ireland came into being.

Although since 1922 Ireland has been politically divided into two parts it is a source of well justified pride to all concerned that in Rotary and Inner Wheel all Ireland is one District, Rotary District 116 — Inner Wheel District No. 16, and that the District has the distinction of special mention in the name — the Association of Inner Wheel Clubs in Great Britain *and Ireland*.

It was not then until 1931 that Mrs. Golding visited Belfast to meet a group of wives of members of the first Belfast Rotary Club. This meeting took place in the home of Mrs. Harris Rundle, who can be called the true pioneer of Inner Wheel in Ireland for as a result of that meeting the first Irish Club formed. This Club was given a green ribbon with their badges, it is recorded, but this was abandoned in favour of the blue one when the Association was formed, though it is said some of the original members clung possessively to the green for some time afterwards — understandably in Ireland! This Belfast Club is one of the '79 ers'.

Under its first President, Lady Turner, the Club devoted its energies to helping to relieve the hardships caused by the industrial depression of the time, particularly by the organising of clothing clubs and soup kitchens in the worst hit areas of Belfast. Then during the war service was switched chiefly to giving assistance to the Red Cross and to the running of canteens at the railway stations and docks.

Not unnaturally no further Clubs formed in Ireland during the war years, but almost as if to make up for lost time, and as if in true Irish spirit impatient to get going, in 1945 Clubs started up in both Ballymena and Larne. It was with these three Clubs as a foundation that No. 16 District was born, a member of the Belfast Club its first Chairman.

It was an auspicious occasion when Mrs. Irene Laycock, the then Association President, attended the luncheon party in the Grand Central Hotel in Belfast to inaugurate the new District and to present the young Clubs of Ballymena and Larne with their Charters, and particularly appropriate too that it should have been Mrs. Laycock, who officiated at the ceremony, for by coming to do so, she was, as it happened, returning to home ground. She had received her education at Victoria College, Belfast.

It could perhaps be said that extension in Ireland has at times been relatively slow, but in all fairness it must be borne in mind that No. 16 District is a very scattered one. Distances combined with difficulties in travel, particularly of recent times, has not facilitated the work of any Extension Organiser. Nevertheless by 1950 five further Clubs were established and in 1967 a happy breakthrough came about with the forming of the first ever Club in Eire, that of Drogheda, followed in 1970 by that of Dublin, and at present there are in all eighteen Clubs in the District.

Vital to the holding together of a District spanning such a wide area as this, was news of each other. Some form of written communication was a necessity. Today the Magazine of No. 16 District admirably fills the need. Its publication dates from 1945, the year of the District's foundation when Mrs. T. Bloomer of the Ballymena Club held the office known then as District Correspondent. It was she who was responsible for making the arrangement with the Editor of 'Cogs' — the Rotary publication in Ireland — that Inner Wheel notes would appear in its pages once in every three months. This arrangement lasted up until 1957 when space became limited and first thought was given to having an independent Inner Wheel News Bulletin. This duly appeared, known as 'The Ulster Wheel' — the cost unbelievably one shilling and threepence for five editions within the Inner Wheel year. Inevitably this number has had to be reduced. In 1963 the number of issues dropped to three per annum. Now two copies only appear annually. The name 'Ulster' was, of course, omitted from the title in 1966 with the happy prospect of further extension throughout the country.

Inner Wheel members in Ireland are very conscious that 'no man is an island'. They keep in the closest possible touch with other Districts by correspondence. Their involvement in overseas work is total, although there are no Zones for this in the District. Neither do they hold Overseas Rallies. In all outward-looking activities, perhaps the more so because they live on an island apart geographically, they demonstrate a great interest in all Association programmes and projects, giving enormous practical help wherever it is needed.

Since 1953 the District has sent representatives to the Standing Conference of Women's Organisations and in this way is kept well informed on all matters of moment. In fact, the Irish Inner Wheel member and perhaps in particular No. 16 District Council Members seem deserving of special mention and regard, for throughout the years they have been most diligent in maintaining the link with the Association, to-ing and fro-ing to Conferences and to meetings held in London with complete disregard for any possible travel hazards. Always they arrive full of good humour, radiating their own particular charm and warmth of friendship, and so it came as no surprise that the Association was blessed with a President from Ireland in 1972 — Mrs. Hylda Armstrong (Coleraine).

Two years later, in July 1974, No. 16 District and indeed the entire Association had further reason to be proud of a great and gifted President for the honorary degree of Doctor of Letters was conferred upon Mrs. Armstrong and in the same year she became the President of International Inner Wheel.

Numerically one of the smaller of Inner Wheel Districts —
maybe so, but No. 16 District has made a vast, incalculable
and wonderful contribution to the organisation.

Well done, Ireland! Maith thú Éire!

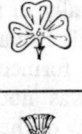

> 'And there's a hand, my trusty fiere,
> And gie's a hand o' thine . . .'
>
> ROBERT BURNS.

Inner Wheel, unlike Hadrian, did not stop short south of
the border into Scotland. It would be untrue, however, to say
it did not encounter any pockets of resistance. Some canny
Scottish Rotarians are known to have held out agin for periods
of as long as thirty and forty-three years! Others, however,
were as only Scotsmen can be, wildly enthusiastic and all for
the lassies doing their own thing, capitulated immediately and
for the most part any warfare in the matter has died out as the
years have passed and now there are not only Inner Wheel
Clubs north of the border but three Districts of them.

The first penetration of Inner Wheel into Scotland was in
fact made by Mrs. Golding herself when she went north in
1930 to address twenty Rotary wives in Paisley. Up until then
these ladies had been meeting fortnightly in each other's
homes for no more an exalted purpose than the enjoyment of
playing cards together. They had, however, it must be added,
been giving any cash left over from these occasions, to local
charities. Together with their husbands they had also been
undertaking many services to the community and at this time
were known as 'THE HUB', but they decided to join Inner
Wheel, thus qualifying to become one of the '79 ers', the only
one in Scotland.

And there infiltration into Scotland might have stopped had
it not been for one greatly dedicated Aberdeen Rotarian and

that Club's President in 1936 — Joseph Bisset, who accompanied by his wife, Alice, attended without fail every Rotary Conference wherever it was held. It was Alice Bisset who determined to start an Inner Wheel Club in Aberdeen. In 1941 she found a staunch ally in the Rotary Club President who called a meeting of all Rotary wives in the city. As a result the Aberdeen Club formed in 1943, Alice Bisset its Founder President. She was not content, however, to let matters rest there. She knew of the Club of Paisley which had manfully been working away on its own for so long, but Paisley was all of one hundred and fifty miles from Aberdeen and there were many towns in between with large, successful Rotary Clubs. Alice Bisset sought help from Mrs. Jessie Park, then Secretary of No. 3 District just over the border, who supplied encouragement and guidance on District formation, and learning that it was necessary that four Clubs should form in Scotland Alice Bisset made this her aim.

Once more a sympathetic Rotary Club of Aberdeen President lent a willing hand, suggesting a Ladies' Day be held in the city to which two Rotary wives from every Club throughout Scotland be invited, no strings attached, but overnight hospitality laid on. It is uncertain now how many ladies accepted but it is known that the towns of Motherwell and Wishaw, Paisley, Edinburgh, Perth, Dunfermline, Stirling, Kirkcaldy, Leven, Elgin, Fraserburgh and Inverness were represented and from that day on Inner Wheel in Scotland blossomed. Immediately Clubs formed in both Perth and Edinburgh. The Founder President of the Perth Club was Mrs. J. E. T. Stewart, still affectionately known throughout the District as 'Jet' Stewart and the Perth Club today is an energetic one in more senses than one, for it has within its membership a lively Country Dancing element. The 'Inner Wheel Jig' is a merry tune composed by a Perth Honorary member and known throughout Scotland and further afield.

The stage was now set for a Scottish District to form and to mark the importance of the occasion the Association President, Mrs. Coote and Mrs. Gladys Young, the Association Secretary, travelled north to Perth which by reason of its central position was a convenient meeting place and there in the Station Hotel, still today, thirty years on, the meeting place of the Perth Club, on September 4th, 1946, in the presence of seventy-four members, District No. 1 and 2 was inaugurated.

The District's Founder Chairman came, appropriately enough, from Aberdeen, Mrs. A. T. Morrison (at time of writing a fit and lively nonagenarian). It was her husband who presented to the District the Chairman's Badge of Office with one proviso, that if the District was ever to divide, the badge would remain in the District which included Aberdeen. The four Founder Clubs were soon joined by others. By 1948 there were thirteen; by 1950 twenty. By then it had become obvious that to serve such a widespread area a Magazine should be available and the first issue of the No. 1 and 2 District Bulletin was printed.

The days of No. 1 and 2 District as such, however, were now numbered. The year was 1951. There were now twenty-three Inner Wheel Clubs in Scotland but Rotary District 1 and 2 was dividing and so the final meeting of the Inner Wheel District took place in Edinburgh where it was decided there would from then on be thirteen Clubs in No. 1 District and ten Clubs in No. 2.

This new No. 1 District found its first Chairman in the Club of Dundee, Mrs. J. A. Davidson, and could not have had a more devoted one. Subsequently the Dundee Club was to supply the District with two more Chairmen, Mrs. I. Malcolm and Mrs. J. C. Pattison, and it was to the latter's home that, as recently as in 1975, a visit was unexpectedly paid by a Norwegian member, Mrs. Margaret Spenning, Chairman of No. 31 District (Norway) in 1974/75. Overseas Links between Scottish and Scandinavian Clubs are strong and hospitality on both sides an outstanding feature, but on this occasion it was to turn out that the link was stronger even than thought, for Mrs. Spenning, a Scot by birth, married to a Norwegian Rotarian, it transpired was incredibly the niece of the Founder Chairman, Mrs. Davidson!

No. 1 District then started all over again with thirteen Clubs but successive Chairmen of the Extension Committee with great diligence and much travelling have more than doubled that number and now in 1976 there is every prospect of more to come. Many of them are, admittedly small, but so, relatively speaking, are the towns, and the distances between considerable. Members undertake tiring journeys to attend even their own Club meetings, one especially intrepid member in the Club of Inverness taking a journey of one hundred miles in her stride. Granted travel problems may not be peculiar to No. 1 District but they do exist there, and members justifiably often feel envious of those in the south who can with much greater ease visit neighbouring Clubs. An effort is made to be fair to all and for District meetings the centres are switched about, some in Perth, some in Aberdeen and more recently some in Aviemore, but even then, members of the most northerly Club in Great Britain and Ireland, that of Wick, require to come by air.

It is a particular source of pride in the District that the member who founded the Forres Club in 1954, Mrs. W. G. Guthrie, more than twenty years later came to hold the high and responsible office of Treasurer for International Inner Wheel.

The District can claim one further distinction — in this instance through Rotary — that in its soil has been bred this year (1976) by an Aberdeen Rotarian rose-grower of international fame, a new and beautiful rose. It is listed as being 'of a bright orange salmon shaded peach yellow'. Surely the loveliest of all compliments which can be paid to a woman is to have a rose bear her name, and this rose has been called 'Jean Thomson Harris' in memory of the wife of Paul Harris, Founder of Rotary.

Members who happen to travel north into Scotland by rail may very well arrive at Waverley Station, Edinburgh, and see writ large on a poster there the unfamiliar-looking words — 'CEUD MILE FAILTE'. Translated they mean 'a hundred thousand welcomes'. They have arrived in the heart of Midlothian, the heart of Inner Wheel No. 2 District.

As a separate entity the District, as we have read, came into being with ten Clubs, with close on four hundred members.

Gradually it extended and by 1964 membership had reached the thousand mark. Geographically District No. 2 encompassed the central industrial belt of Scotland, extended north west to Oban and southwards to the Borders. The first District Meeting after the division was held in Glasgow under the Chairmanship of Mrs. A. Gardiner of the old established Paisley Club.

A very interesting feature of this District's history is that the Edinburgh Club had as its first Honorary Member, the wife of the Rotary Founder, Mrs. Paul Harris. It came about this way. The Founder President of the Edinburgh Club, Mrs. W. Winkler and her Committee, knowing that Jean Thomson Harris had been born and bred in the city, decided that she should be invited to become an Honorary Member. Replying to Mrs. Winkler from her home in Chicago in 1946, Mrs. Harris wrote immediately accepting, adding — 'I have been keeping in touch with Inner Wheel activities through the Rotary Service Magazine. Paul and I are amazed and thrilled at the magnitude of its benefactions. It seems miraculous after all you have been through. (Meaning the war years.) May God bless your every endeavour.'

Without Paul Harris — no Rotary movement. Without Rotary — no Inner Wheel, and so as wives of Rotarians it is only natural to be curious about, and want to learn something of this woman who was the wife of the first Rotarian. Jean Thomson was born in 1881, the second daughter of a family of four boys and four girls. She was a good-looking, attractive girl who early in life chose to work for a time as a lady's maid in the households of several well-known Scottish families. Such experience enabled her in later life to mix easily with people from all ranks of society. But how, we want to know, was it, that a young Scots girl of that time came to be in Chicago, where to meet and marry Paul Harris who was a rising young lawyer there?

It seems that two of her brothers and a sister emigrated to Canada and Jean elected to follow to keep house for them. In 1905 she became a member of a rambling club, a popular leisure-time activity with young people in those days. It was in this way she met her husband-to-be. In 1910 they were married. In 1912 they moved into a house that was to be their home for the rest of their married life. They called it 'Comely Bank' after the district in Edinburgh in which Jean had spent her early years. There was no family and so it was that Mrs. Harris was free to accompany her husband on his travels in the development of the Rotary movement. In 1934 they visited Edinburgh, attended a weekly luncheon meeting of the Edinburgh Club, received a tremendous welcome and were presented with a silver salver as a memento of the occasion.

For many years after Paul died in 1947 Jean Harris continued to give much voluntary service in the city of Chicago, but eventually she felt a strong desire to return to her native land. This she did and although she never actually attended any meetings of Inner Wheel she generously contributed annually to the Edinburgh Club's charity fund. In 1963 she died just after her eighty-second birthday. And here a most remarkable and hitherto unknown circumstance came to light quite by chance when genealogical research was being undertaken into the whereabouts of her grave. She is buried in Newington Cemetery, Dalkeith Road, Edinburgh, only some few paces from the burial ground of the writer's own maternal great grand-parents. A modest headstone there marks the grave of Jean Thomson Harris, the wife and helpmeet of the man to whom all our members owe so much.

In the year 1971 No. 2 District was to divide into Districts No. 2 and 23. By then it had a total of forty-two Clubs, and was celebrating its twenty-first birthday. It commenced its new existence with twenty-one Clubs and the first District Meeting took place in Edinburgh under the Chairmanship of Mrs. R. McLean of the Denny Club. And so once again a new chapter began for No. 2 District. Extension in it has barely had time to happen and the transferring of Clubs into the new No. 23 District has diminished it numerically, but it has a long and strong tradition to sustain its future.

District No. 23 — this healthy offspring of No. 2 District has within its boundaries twenty-four Clubs of greatly diverse size and background, those of the large, industrial centres such as Glasgow, Greenock and Clydebank and those of the small, picturesque watering places such as Lochgilphead and Ayr. Progress in the District has been steady rather than spectacular but actual membership has increased of late, and it was an especial joy to the District to welcome the Club of Girvan nearly twenty years after the formation of the town's Rotary Club. It is with pride too, that this comparatively new District has already given to the Association a Vice-President for 1976/77 in the person of Mrs. W. Petitt (Dumbarton), the first ever Scot to be elected to that office.

No history of this young District would be complete either without mention of the tremendous enjoyment and friendly rivalry which exists between its members and those of No. 2 District socially. Annually they meet and contend for sporting trophies and in this way friendships of past years are kept alive.

For easy reference, Scotland as a whole, incorporating the re-formation of Districts there since 1946 up until the present has been dealt with. Now we must revert to 1947 and come back over the border into No. 19 District and it seems Inner Wheel in Great Britain and Ireland has turned full circle for this District was born out of the second division of the oldest one, No. 5. It started life with a goodly inheritance of already formed, thriving Clubs, twenty-two of them and six of their number '79 ers' — Nelson and Blackburn (both 1928); Blackpool (1929); Preston (1932); and Accrington and Rossendale (both 1934). The first District meeting was held in Lancaster with every Club represented and it is on record that a gavel was presented to the young District by its mother one (presumably to keep its offspring in order!).

As a further bonus the District had the good fortune to have as its Founder Chairman, Mrs. Millicent Gaskell, who in the previous year had been Chairman of No. 5 District. With such beginnings success and growth was assured, and in fact before the first year was out two further Clubs had formed, one at

Grange-over-Sands and one in Douglas, Isle of Man (now in No. 5 District). Extension has steadily forged ahead and now in 1976 the number of Clubs has more than doubled the original figure.

In 1949 Mrs. Millicent Gaskell was elected Association President and later in 1953 an Association Treasurer, Mrs. L. Pickles (Nelson) was provided by the District.

No one will grudge here special mention being made of the Blackpool Club. Of course, it is by a happy accident of geographical position that it is an attribute to No. 19 District, and has acted as Hostess Club at so many Annual Conferences, but it is a large Club with a large heart. It meets fortnightly and from studying its records there emerges a chronicle of service given in all sorts of ways peculiar to a seaside resort of such size and repute; the organising of summer hospitality for the elderly, for sick children, for convalescents, for all-comers in fact, including ourselves, and each Association President in turn when the Conference is held in the town, humbly tries to express gratitude. 'We have only to ask to receive,' said Association President Jessie Moon in 1976. How very true!

Districts No. 20, 21, 22 and 23 — all are comparatively new (for No. 23 District see Scotland). All were created in 1972 and No. 24, youngest of all, in 1974. Consequently they have little history of their own as yet, but they are rapidly making it. Most have fallen heir to Clubs which are old and experienced. In No. 20 District, for example, in which there were to begin with, twenty-eight Clubs, twenty from No. 10 District; four from No. 11 and four from No. 17, there are already thirty Clubs and from the Shepton Mallet one, transferred there after many years' service to both her original Club of Putney and to No. 13 District came the Association President for 1975/76.

It would be glossing over the truth to imply that with division, boundaries for Districts have presented no problems; they have. And some may not as yet be satisfactorily resolved, but in the instances where travel difficulties, particularly with regard to attendance at District Meetings, have arisen and notice of the circumstances has been brought to the attention of the Council, it has always been given full and sympathetic consideration. (The map overleaf shows present District boundaries which follow those of Districts in Rotary.)

And thus — outlined in as much detail as space in this history will allow — the Association of Inner Wheel Clubs in Great Britain and Ireland has gone — NATIONWIDE.

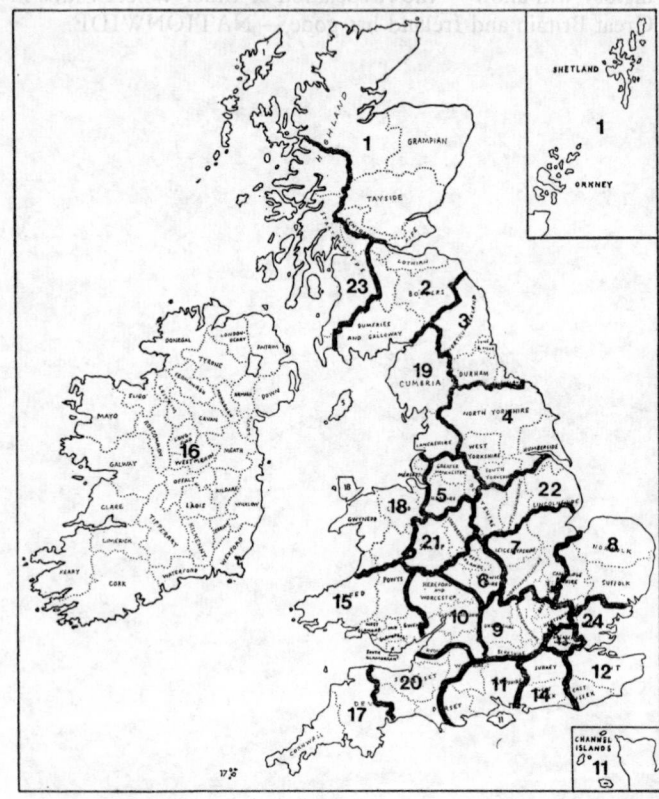

Going Global

BECAUSE this is primarily a history book it would seem appropriate to begin at least one part of it in a traditional manner and as this very important chapter in the life of Inner Wheel contains such an element of chance — it has indeed a story-book quality about it — we begin by saying that . . .

Once upon a time there was a man, a travelling man who in truth builded better than he knew. He lived in the town of Ballarat, Australia, which in those days was not simply a two-day jet flight away. Nevertheless he journeyed to England. (It is perhaps unnecessary to mention he was a Rotarian, a member of the Ballarat Club formed in 1925.) Arrived in England he heard of Inner Wheel, liked what he heard, made it his business to obtain some details of how it functioned, in the course of time returned to his home town and told Rotary wives there what it was all about. They too liked what they heard and so it came to pass that in 1931 after a Rotary Conference in Ballarat, a cable was despatched by that Rotary Club's President, Rotarian L. Maddern, to Mrs. Golding who by post advised and guided and as a result the Inner Wheel Club of Ballarat was formed.

The first years in the life of the Ballarat Club were productive of much effort. Listed, in fact, is support for no less than seventeen local community organisations, including help given to one of particular significance in Australia, a Bush Fire Relief Appeal. Came the Second World War and Club members undertook the sending of many parcels of comforts to the United Kingdom, in particular ones containing knitted garments, using wool made available by U.N.R.R.A., to the Club of Birkenhead, England, and as the years passed the Ballarat Club was to sponsor several other Inner Wheel Clubs. In this way Inner Wheel put down first roots in the southern hemisphere where, we have good reason for saying, especially now in 1976, with the third International Inner Wheel Convention having been held in Sydney, New South Wales, it has lived happy ever after.

The first entry of Inner Wheel into the continent of Europe is another story, equally short, equally simple and involving yet again Mrs. Golding who, receiving a postal enquiry from the wife of a Norwegian Rotarian, Mrs. John Irminger of Bergen, undertook to supply details of how the movement operated. The ensuing correspondence resulted in the forming with twenty members on April 1st, 1935, of the Bergen Inner Wheel Club, destined to be the only Inner Wheel Club on the continent for ten years, many of them years of war when its existence in occupied territory was put in jeopardy.

In 1940 Rotary in Bergen was forbidden. Inner Wheel found it advisable to dissolve *officially*, but with great courage members continued to meet in secret in each other's homes, ostensibly to play bridge, in reality to find stimulus in friendships shared and, with money donated by Rotary when it ceased to exist, to buy wool with which to knit, materials with which to sew. As conditions worsened greater grew their resolve and resistance. Food was hidden away in members' homes for distribution to children at Christmas. Children whose parents had been imprisoned were 'adopted' and when in 1944 a great explosion with devastating fires occurred in the town, it is recorded that members, using foodstuffs secretly stored away produced between three and five thousand sandwiches daily for distribution to hospitals.

This struggle to survive as a Club regardless, merited recognition and reward and it came. The President of the Association in Great Britain and Ireland managed to send through the Red Cross a message of encouragement and greeting of which later Mrs. Irminger was to write — 'It was like a friendly handshake from across the sea. It had words which warmed our hearts.' Happier days have come for those worthy Norwegian members, much happier times for Inner Wheel in that country, for today there are five Districts there.

The third and last short story we tell here of the beginnings of Inner Wheel overseas concerns four Rotarians and their wives who, immediately after World War II chose to take a continental holiday, not a remarkable circumstance in itself, but one which was to have great consequence. The gentlemen were members of the Rotary Club of Hayes and Harlington formed in 1935, their ladies members of the Hayes and Harlington Inner Wheel Club, No. 13 District, which had formed rather daringly considering its vulnerable position in the war years. The Club is regrettably no longer with us, but it left Inner Wheel a treasured legacy, for the party travelled to Holland, to the town of Apeldoorn.

We have no details of that visit but it must have been enjoyed on both sides for a return visit was arranged for the Dutch Rotarians and their wives. The wives saw how the Hayes and Harlington Club functioned and returned home to form at Apeldoorn the first Inner Wheel Club in the Netherlands. Two years on, in 1948, what does the now thriving Club of Apeldoorn do, but call upon the further six Clubs which had formed in that short time in The Netherlands to form a District. It was the first District to form outside of Great Britain and Ireland and looking back we salute those concerned, for the formation of any District anywhere in the world has always been looked upon as a triumph in our history.

These three instances illustrate one thing in particular — how the approach to become part of Inner Wheel overseas has always come from 'outside'. There never was any planned project to form clubs. They simply happened as a result of individual or group enquiry. All the more remarkable was it, therefore, that by 1945 all of fifteen Clubs had emerged in parts of the world as far apart as in South Africa and Canada, New Zealand and America, all entirely of their own free will.

With correspondence their only link with the Association not unnaturally some of the Clubs which had formed in remote places felt the need for a closer liaison. The Club of Port Elizabeth, South Africa, felt so strongly about this that it applied by letter in 1945 for a Charter of Affiliation. To this plea the Association at once responded by sending out a letter to all of the fifteen Clubs, asking if they wished to become affiliated. This was a bold stroke on the part of the Association, for if those fifteen Clubs had refused to accept the rules and constitution as binding upon them they could have been lost to the movement for all time. Mercifully, however, agreement was almost total.

As was to be expected this affiliation brought changes, the first very necessary one being dealt with at the first post-war Conference when the title of the Association was altered to read simply — 'The Association of Inner Wheel Clubs', the words 'Great Britain and Ireland' being dropped. There were also financial aspects of moment to be settled without delay. Currency regulations in some countries forbade the paying of capitation fees which meant that members of Clubs in those countries would have no vote in the making of rules which they were obliged to keep. Obviously this in all fairness had somehow to be sorted out. Now it has always been an Inner Wheel policy that each member should have a say in the work of a Club; that as many Clubs as possible should take part in the work of a District and that through the Districts the administration of the Association should be arrived at, and so in order to deal with the situation which had now arisen it was deemed advisable that a committee made up of members with specialised knowledge on this score should be set up. Three such Ad Hoc Committees were in fact set up, the first in 1952 which only met once, the second in 1956 and the third in 1958.

In 1956 the Officers of No. 26 District (The Netherlands) which it will be remembered had been the first overseas District to form, invited the President and five other members to visit them with a view to discussing administrative problems arising from the growth of the movement overseas. As a result of this visit, composed of the members who had gone to the Netherlands, the second Ad Hoc Committee formed — 'To consider the present and future status of Clubs overseas with special reference to control, representation and obligations.' This led to the drafting of a letter sent to all overseas Clubs suggesting that if they were prepared to pay capitation fees it would entitle them to representation for constitutional business at the Annual Conference in person or by proxy. (The currency regulations had been altered by then and permitted

66

payment of these.) Around seventy-five per cent of the Clubs agreed without question. The necessary constitutional changes were made at the Annual Conference in 1957 and in the following year these new powers were exercised, approximately fifty per cent of overseas Clubs voting which was encouraging to all concerned. The third Ad Hoc Committee then got to work to put on record the growth and development of Inner Wheel Clubs and Districts overseas from the formation of the first Club onwards, this bearing in mind advice given by Past Association President Mrs. Coote, that early events and reasons for them became lost unless recorded.

All this had occasioned a great deal of work and responsibility on the part of those Association Officers in charge at the time and numerous other relevant matters kept cropping up to which they had to give attention. It had been discovered, for example, that unofficial Clubs using the name 'Inner Wheel' were in operation in various parts of the world. They were sent invitations to affiliate. If the invitation was rejected they had to be informed that the Association took no responsibility for their activities. It was necessary to have Club and District Rule Books translated into several languages. All manner of further minor adjustments had in fact to be arranged, but it was all so very worth while for new Clubs were forming fast. They had started in Belgium, France, Denmark and Sweden and by 1960 Inner Wheel had gone much, much further afield. It had reached out into India, Israel, North Borneo (Sabah), Uganda, Ghana and Finland, totalling almost two hundred in ten Districts.

The year 1962 saw another major step taken towards worldwide unification. An Ad Hoc Committee set out to consider ways and means of giving Clubs and Districts overseas some measure in the administration of the Association and at the Annual Conference that year their recommendations were approved — that a District no matter where in the world situated should have the same rights as a District in Great Britain and Ireland; that it should have a representative on the Governing Body of the Association with the right to nominate members to serve as Association Officers and the right to vote in person at the election of Association Officers. The vision of a truly International Inner Wheel was rapidly coming clearer. A period of three years was suggested as a suitable time in which to enable Districts overseas to gain first-hand experience of how the Association worked. At the end of this period it was hoped to plan a broad basis for the establishment of International Inner Wheel and, in fact, that is exactly what happened.

The Annual Conference in 1966 was held in Blackpool. It rained that year, if we remember rightly, but nothing could extinguish the expectancy, the feeling of excitement, the already *international* aura. Coincidentally but appropriately enough it was at this Conference that the colourful 'Dolls of the world' Exhibition was held and on the Agenda for the Business meeting appeared the promisingly worded proposal put forward by the Governing Body — 'That an International Association should be formed to operate as from July 1st, 1967'. Unnecessary to add the proposal was carried and that members all automatically from that date became members of International Inner Wheel. What in effect had happened was that a fourth level of administration had come into being — Club, District, Association, International Inner Wheel.

The foregoing is the very briefest of accounts, a summary, indeed an abridgement of all that occurred, for there were countless ramifications, not the least of which were the ever-important necessary financial adjustments which required immediate attention and these fell upon the shoulders of the Association Treasurer of the time and members of the Finance Committee. To each country which would now be forming an Association, i.e., those with a representative on the International Board, had to be allocated a fair proportion of the monies in hand. This division called for financial expertise. Solicitors and Auditors had to be consulted. To send such monies out of the country Bank of England permission had to be sought, but in the end, to quote the Association Treasurer responsible — 'Everything went very smoothly'.

Inevitably going global has meant more expense which is reflected in every single member's contribution. Against this we must balance in our minds, and even more in our hearts, the worthiness of the concept. Has it been worth it? Is it worth it? The answer comes unbidden and surely unchallenged. Clearly yes, if the movement has to have any meaning at all throughout the land, *our* land and *their* lands. As soon as International Inner Wheel became fact we ceased forever indeed to think like that — in terms of 'we' and 'they'. Someone once remarked that 'the language of distress is international' and mindful of that, and the aims and objects originally laid down for Inner Wheel to be of service wherever there is need the organisation has become one united universal body.

Voting world-wide at the 1967 Conference in Brighton brought into office those members destined to guide International Inner Wheel in its first years. They were Mrs. D. M. Weightman (G.B. & I.), the first President; Mrs. M. Foster (G.B. & I.), Vice-President, and Mrs. J. Casson (G.B. & I.) the first Treasurer. Only to begin with were the reins of office to be in the hands of members from Great Britain and Ireland, however, and rightly so. In 1970 Mrs. E. Bager (Sweden) became President. Mrs. C. W. N. Sharp (G.B. & I.) followed in 1971. Mrs. B. Fangel (Denmark) 1972; Mrs. M. Bulpitt (G.B. & I.) 1973; Dr. H. Armstrong (G.B. & I.) 1974; Mrs. R. E. Davies (Australia) 1975; and in 1976 Mrs. M. C. Cronstedt (Sweden).

It was at this 1967 Conference too, that members from the Scandinavian countries — Norway, Sweden, Denmark and The Netherlands — who had worked so assiduously towards the establishing of International Inner Wheel during the previous five years, made the generous gesture of adding to the presidential regalia by presenting the gift of a specially designed link bracelet. The bracelet was symbolic of their wish that the links of friendship now so firmly established would be forever as close and indeed they have been ever since.

The function of the International Board is to keep the entire organisation together as the Association in Great Britain and Ireland did up until 1967. It is no easy assignment, for although recent technological advance has greatly increased the ease and speed with which contact can be made and it seems that the world is shrinking daily, it is still a big place and within Inner Wheel there are many as yet non-districted Clubs, some of which are likely to remain so. They plough a lonely furrow and command high regard. They cannot enjoy the rapport as

Club meets Club at District meetings, nor experience the incentive that exchanging views personally delegate with delegate brings, but each and every one of them is as important in the scheme of things as those who have those advantages.

In her address to the Annual Conference in 1976 in Great Britain and Ireland, International Inner Wheel President, Mrs. R. E. Davies, graphically illustrated the value of the individual member and no doubt she had in mind too those non-districted Clubs, many of them in her own country. When thinking of members world-wide and of the things they achieved in the name of Inner Wheel she was often reminded, she said, of a cartoon she had once seen which depicted a plain bar of iron valued at five pounds. When made into horseshoes its value was ten pounds, fifty pence. If made into needles it would have been worth three thousand, two hundred and fifty pounds and if turned into balance springs for watches its worth became one quarter of a million pounds. The same was true, she concluded, of the Inner Wheel member wherever in the world she was.

Ways do exist, however, of keeping in touch with even the most remote of Clubs. The Link Scheme started in Great Britain and Ireland in 1961 though no longer official still prospers in many places through correspondence, the exchange of photographs and in some instances now by tapes sent and avidly listened to at Club meetings. In her year in office the International Inner Wheel President conscientiously, her time and available finances permitting, travels to the countries where and when it seems most appropriate she should. This calls for much forethought in programming. And all members are by now familiar with the International Inner Wheel Magazine. Some editions of this have borne on the front cover the drawing of a single rose, the emblem of true friendship in many continental countries and, of course, the national flower of England where Inner Wheel originated. This Magazine started life as simply a middle-page insertion in the Magazine of the Association in Great Britain and Ireland in 1968, its first editor Mrs. M. Foster, who also held the office then of Vice-President. In that first issue Mrs. Foster included a description of International Inner Wheel Headquarters at 27 Three Kings

Yard, London W.1. International Inner Wheel is still housed there, where members visiting London are always made to feel welcome. Although now an entirely separate publication, the Magazine is neither an ambitious nor elaborate production on account of the strictest economy, but it aims to carry news of Inner Wheel Clubs the world over.

Speaking of International Inner Wheel and her hopes for it back in 1966, Mrs. D. M. Weightmann, who was then President of the Association in Great Britain and Ireland, said: 'In due course I hope we will have Conventions.' Her hopes have been realised. In 1970 the first of them was held in The Netherlands at the Hague, the occasion graced by the presence of Her Majesty Queen Juliana. In 1973 the second International Convention took place in Copenhagen when Her Majesty Queen Ingrid of Denmark honoured it by being present. The third Convention in 1976 was the first to be held outside of Europe, said to be the largest gathering of women ever to be held in the Southern Hemisphere, the venue for it was Sydney, Australia. So — in its short life, International Inner Wheel has turned full circle, for it will be remembered the first overseas Club ever to form was that of Ballarat.

Couched in the simplest terms for brevity's sake this mere outline of the setting up of International Inner Wheel might with some justice be accused of over-simplification. In correcting any such impression it is very necessary to say that the process was anything but simple. It was a long haul fraught with many pitfalls and complications, the goal of international unification being reached only after years of serious application on the part of not only members in Great Britain and Ireland — for all members had a voice in its shaping — but members from overseas who gave equally of their time and thought to the enormity of the project, for despite Shakespeare a girdle cannot yet be put round about the earth in forty minutes. That is only a midsummer night's dream. It took Inner Wheel over forty *years* to realise the dream of its Founder, but even at that the mind boggles. Look back for a moment . . . Manchester, England in 1924, one Club, in it a mere handful of women. Today in 1976, close on two thousand Clubs throughout the world with some sixty thousand members.

Of No Fixed Abode

DURING all of the early years Inner Wheel in Great Britain
and Ireland led a singularly nomadic existence office-wise. An
organisation as numerically strong as it had become by 1934
very obviously required a base camp from which to conduct
its affairs, but it had none. Intermittently references to the fact
that the subject came up for discussion are to be found, but
always such major expense as would have been involved
appears to have been deemed unwise and the matter shelved.
This may or may not have been the right policy. Some have
accused our Founders of overdoing the prudence, but it is not
useful to be clever after a passage of time. Suffice it to say that
our early administrators wished to keep running costs to a
minimum in the interest of all members and so from the
formation of the Association right up to 1949 no headquarters known as such existed. All business was carried out
firstly by Mrs. Mabel Nixon and then by Mrs. Gladys Young,
both working from their homes, with latterly, a young office
girl employed at a salary of one hundred pounds per annum,
to assist Mrs. Young. What is more, all the Association
possessed in the way of equipment was one typewriter and one
filing cabinet purchased in 1938, neither by the time ten years
had passed of any value whatsoever — this then when membership had climbed into the region of twelve thousand.

Plainly such a totally inadequate arrangement could not
continue. Daily the paper work mounted. What was needed
was a central office and a full-time secretary, and so in September 1949 furnished premises were found to rent at 1a Marylebone Road, London, N.W.1, and the first paid Secretary, Miss
Elizabeth Eaton was engaged. It was a very modest beginning
and, as it turned out, a very temporary one too, for by the end of
the year we had been asked to make alternative arrangements.

Photograph by Rotarian Clifford Moon.

51 Warwick Square, London, S.W.1.

Photograph by Rotarian Clifford Moon.

The Functions Board in the Secretary's room.

Photograph by Rotarian Clifford Moon.

In the General Office, from left to right: Mrs. Barbara Buchan, Mrs. Carol Clarke and Miss Jane Dobson.

The need to find other accommodation within the first twelve months was a blow and a set-back, but after a difficult search, a move was made in the spring of 1950 into part of the W.V.S. Club in Cadogan Square, S.W.1. There are not all that many members around now who remember working there, but Mrs. E. H. McKellen Wild, who was Association President 1952/53, writing in 1959 recalled how pleasant it was — 'in the Committee room at the top of the building; the windows open to the summer air; the distant hum of traffic . . .' And Miss Eaton reported that there had been a considerable number of visiting members calling in and even some from overseas. So it was evident both Officers and members appreciated having headquarters to call their own, but . . . In 1955 the W.V.S. Club there closed and we were homeless once more.

The next move was to 19 Grosvenor Place, S.W.1. The stay there was short-lived, however, for two years later accommodation in Rotary House in Portman Square, W.1, was offered. This, it was thought, was too good an opportunity to be missed. Gladly the offer was accepted and there we were happily housed until 1961 when, Rotary House having been sold for conversion to an embassy, once more we were *of no fixed abode.*

It seemed indeed that the Association was destined never to have settled, suitable and satisfactory headquarters. All this chopping and changing within the span of a few years was undesirable, confusing for members at a distance, not to say awkward in the recruiting and retaining of staff and it involved expense. The next address was 89/91 Newman Street, W.1. Originally a private house, the property had been carved up, and we were accommodated on the fourth floor. There was a private flat opposite the office; on other floors commercial enterprises and although the best available at the time, the premises were really inadequate and inconvenient, but there we remained for six years, the longest period yet in any one place.

It was in 1967 that we heard of accommodation to rent within Berners Hotel, W.1. It sounded desirable and we were on the move again, the actual removal organised by our present Secretary, Miss Jane Dobson. The four-roomed office with toilet and miniscule kitchen was situated at the rear of the

73

building. It was relatively quiet there, compact and comfortable, but it is a salutary fact often learned the hard way that it is necessary to live in a house over a period of time before becoming aware of its shortcomings; likewise with any office. The compactness was too much; the rooms when equipped too little, and they proved extremely un-getatable those rooms. One Association Committee member on a first visit, arriving in a state of near exhaustion, observed that finding the office was like burrowing along tortuous corridors like Alice in Wonderland to find it was always round the next corner. Also, in order to have elbow-room, often members of committees were forced to withdraw to their bedrooms, there to cradle files and card indexes on their knees, of which necessity the same member said — 'We worked, perched on the beds like sparrows on a line.'

These inadequacies and inconveniences were persevered with cheerfully, however, by all the Presidents, Executives and Committee members of the time who were called upon to work there, for there were certain compensations. The hotel was centrally situated; the shops handy; Bourne and Hollingworths just across the street where to snatch a hasty meal or purchase a necessary notebook, replace a lost Biro, and the fact that members travelling from afar could and did stay overnight *within* the hotel was to some extent a boon, for it meant that they could and very often did work on, far into the night, without having to 'shut shop' at any particular hour.

The fact that no lease had ever been granted to the Association for these premises was a cause for concern as time went on. There was a disquieting feeling of unease about the situation, not exactly one of impending doom perhaps, but one of impermanence, probably engendered by past experience. Was it on the cards that, at little notice, we might be asked to vacate? It was and we were. The then owners Grand Metropolitan Hotels Ltd., asked us to make other arrangements.

To say this turn in events put the Association in a serious quandary would be the grossest of understatements. The timing was the worst possible; the year 1972; the London property market in a state of flux; gazumping rampant. Appealed to, Rotary regretfully could see no way to help.

74

Individual members resident in London made countless unavailing enquiries on our behalf. The question was posed — why stay in London necessarily? Why not move into the provinces? The area under scrutiny was immediately widened to encompass Midland cities and some even further afield. It was established that property prices were no lower there, nor suitable premises more available, and in any event, the then Finance Committee under the superb leadership of the Association Treasurer, Mrs. J. Pyke, had gone painstakingly into the matter of costs relative to bringing members of Council and Association Committee members to meetings in cities other than London. Their findings were that overall costs would be greater and inconvenience certainly so. There was also to be considered the question of, by moving out of London, losing knowledgeable, competent and loyal staff, few in number certainly, but the more valuable for that.

The search in London was therefore intensified and tribute must be recorded to those Association Officers who undertook to find premises, come hell or high water, premises to suit our purse and purpose. The Association President was then Mrs. Hylda Armstrong; the Vice-President, Mrs. E. F. L. McCready and Mrs. J. Pyke, the Association Treasurer, who tells of the exact position with which we were faced. 'Little had we anticipated that we would be given notice to quit the offices at the end of June 1972 and would have to be out within six months. At that time we had a year's working balance in hand, plus approximately £10,000 towards future premises. We were given permission by Council to look for somewhere at approximately £5,000 per annum rental, but our difficulty was to find premises to which we would have access after six or seven p.m. as many of the Committees work until very late in order to save another day's expense. Also, as all rented premises are subject to a rental review at intervals, if we rented, we would have no security of a fixed rental. We could then have been placed in a position of paying increased rental or having to find yet again new offices with all the costs consequent upon moving.'

So indefatigably the search went on, necessitating much weary footslogging and frustration for those three members in the viewing of possibles. Househunting at the best of times and purely on one's own account can be trying. How much more onerous and responsible the task of vetting offices in the best interests of all present and future members of an organisation of the size of Inner Wheel in Great Britain and Ireland!

Finally, through the good offices of a member of Council we were given first option on premises which had not yet come on the open market. They were so ideal that it was felt the possibility of buying a ninety-seven years' lease should be investigated without delay. They were self-contained those premises and as such were as scarce as grass in Piccadilly! Our future whereabouts now really were hanging in the balance. It was crucial to find somewhere fast. The time was unfortunate for decision-making. It was the month of August and the majority of Clubs throughout the country in recess, but if we were not to miss the chance, action as near immediate as no matter was called for.

A special meeting of Council was called and those members, many on holiday, were contacted by various means, instantly left for London and it is greatly to their credit that every District was represented. Each Council member took part in a conducted tour of the property, took time out to consider carefully the pros and cons and after much deliberation finally agreement was reached by an overwhelming majority to the proposed purchase, the Finance Committee recommending that it should be financed by the sum of £15,000 being paid out of the Premises Fund and General Reserve Accounts, and the balance of the purchase price to be met by members at £2 per head. This would make it possible to pay for all legal and removal costs out of the money raised. We also had the benefit of an interest free loan of £4,000 when our interest rates were at their highest and based on a day to day basis.

From observation throughout many years now one thing is abundantly clear. The Association has never indulged in any unnecessary spending and this decision, it cannot be emphasised too strongly to purchase a ninety-seven years' lease of No. 51 Warwick Square, London, S.W.1, at a cost of £70,000 was not taken lightly. It was an investment and a sound one. An independent valuation at the time gave a figure of £85,600.

The lease was signed and the date for removal decided upon.

It was perhaps to be expected that it would take some time to convince all members of the wisdom of the purchase, and it did. We had survived all these years without owning property, it was argued, why buy now when the time was anything but favourable for property purchase? And the matter of a £2 per capita levy was not immediately accepted by all. From various quarters were heard rumblings of discontent, even disapproval. Letters of objection were received, culminating in the lively debate witnessed during the Annual General Meeting at the 1973 Conference, but at the end of the day members saw reason and General Resolution No. 2 on the Agenda, proposed by Council which read — 'That whereas the Association of Inner Wheel Clubs in Great Britain and Ireland had purchased the lease of Suite G/H, 51 Warwick Square, London, S.W.1, for a period of ninety-seven years, this Conference shall additionally be asked to ratify the decision of the Association Council for a £2 per capita levy, due for payment before 30th June, 1973, on all Active, Honoured and Honorary Members to meet the cost of the said purchase. V.A.T. will be imposed on levy payments received after 31st March, 1973, and the Club making such payments will be responsible therefor.' — was carried by an overwhelming majority.

Once more our removal was successfully organised by the Association Secretary, Miss Dobson, who tells wryly of her dismay when in order to get certain pieces of office equipment out of Berners Hotel, it was decided by the removal firm to lower them out of an upstairs window into the street below rather than negotiate them along the aforementioned tortuous corridors!

And so at this point in our history, and at long last, the Association of Inner Wheel Clubs in Great Britain and Ireland finally and proudly acquired permanent Headquarters.

TODAY

TODAY

A Home of Our Own

IT is the year 1976. In the quiet tree-lined corner of South West London which is Warwick Square, are the Headquarters, so sorely needed for so very long. A small, unassuming plaque on the right of the doorway says simply 'The Association of Inner Wheel Clubs in Great Britain and Ireland'. The premises are in no way elaborate. They are in fact, strictly functional but exceedingly pleasant, and now that four years have passed it can safely be claimed the settling in period is over and the offices are both well-equipped and fully furnished due to the quite unbelievable generosity of very many Rotarians, of Districts, Clubs and countless individual members. From the moment of taking possession it was as if all wanted to have a stake in making the place truly their own, as if a bride had been asked to supply a suggestion list of wedding presents. From all over the country there flooded in, not just pieces of good furniture, fine china, glassware, pictures and such refinements, but all manner of domestic necessities, so much so that eventually the gift list had to be declared closed.

Not that everything there is new. All about are reminders of the past. Many are the items given to the Association long ago in memory of past members and many are the reminders that the organisation is international, among the latter the silver boomerang from Australia and the illuminated plaques from South Africa.

The tile-floored entrance hall is wide, light, uncluttered. All the walls are cream-painted. On the right-hand one hangs the oaken board upon which appear in gilt the names of all Association Past Presidents, this board presented years ago now by No. 14 District in memory of one of the District's Past Secretaries, Mrs. W. F. Rees. On either side of this are draped two wall-hangings of deep blue felt to which are attached handsomely and elaborately worked Banners from Clubs all over the world.

The General Office looks out on to the Square, under its two windows carefully tended pot-plants, the only purely ornamental touch, for although it is a spacious room, necessary office equipment occupies most of the floor space. In this room hangs the clock presented to the Association in memory of Association President Mrs. H. H. Coote by her District. The door opposite is that leading into the Board Room in which at some time in every week assemble either members of the Executive Committee or of other Association Committees. Here is the Presidential Chair, a gift from No. 13 District in memory of Mrs. W. A. Shakerley, Association President back in 1936. Behind it on the wall is a large portrait of Mrs. Oliver Golding, a constant reminder of Inner Wheel beginnings and all who have occasion to work in this room hope she regards them with a tolerant and understanding eye for times and circumstances have changed so since her time.

In the rear of the building the Secretary's private office is situated; a red-carpeted, cheerful, business-like room this, dominated on the far wall by the eye-catching, useful Functions Board showing throughout the year events, so that at a glance it can be seen what is happening day by day within the world of Inner Wheel in Great Britain and Ireland. This was a gift to the Association from Mrs. Jessie Casson, Association Treasurer between 1963 and 1966. Every square inch of this room has been put to the best possible use; stationery supplies at hand on superb steel shelving; cabinets and cupboards ranged round the walls housing irreplaceable archives, Minute Books from the earliest days and District Histories.

Downstairs, tucked away from all the busyness of the working areas is what has become known as the 'Friendship Room'. Brightly curtained, carpeted in deep blue, furnished with easy chairs, desks and bookshelves, this is a many-purpose room. It is used on occasion by Association Committee members with some task in hand which demands study and quiet. At other times it serves as a homely, comfortable place in which visiting members may meet to chat, or it can answer as a withdrawing room, a bolt-hole for perhaps a travel-weary Association President, somewhere to which she can retreat to snatch a few moments to herself during a brief whistle-stop call at Headquarters before proceeding to her next appointment. Included in the room's tasteful furnishings is the unique beautifully worked tapestry map of the Netherlands, dated 1953 and here live the photograph albums recording all major events in each Association President's year in office and the magnificent pale blue and gold one picturing all Past Association Presidents from Mrs. Golding on, the later photographs in colour. Here too is the handsome green book, souvenir of the Winston Churchill Memorial Statue Appeal, launched in 1970, in it all of eight pages devoted to the names of those Inner Wheel Clubs which contributed. To leaf through all these can be a nostalgic, pleasurable experience. Inner Wheel memories are here for all.

There is too the bonus of a garden which members are not asked to keep in order, which is refreshing. That no one ever has time to wander in it does not diminish the amenity for it is right there, just outside the front door and on one occasion at least it is known to have served a purpose — on a summer day when sandwiches had comprised a Committee's lunch with no break from work (a general practice this to save time) and an Association President, admitting to a feeling of exhaustion, chose to take a brief walk there. Rather naturally in the surroundings the conversation turned to the wonderful effort Clubs throughout the country had made in 1973 to the planting of trees for the pleasure of those living in homes for the elderly, in tree-less precincts and unlovely areas. On arriving back at the gate and carefully locking it (which must be done) that President said smilingly: 'That was refreshing. I feel rejuvenated and ready to start work again!'.

'Regulars' who use 51 Warwick Square as a meeting place include the Club of Westminster East; No. 13 District for meetings of its Executives, Publications and Overseas Service Committees and occasionally too, members from No. 12 and No. 14 Districts have found it a convenient venue. Headquarters have, in fact, very quickly become a Mecca for all members, many on holiday in London making a visit there a 'must'. In one single day visitors from many countries can arrive and all are made immensely welcome by the small, competent and ever cheerful staff. Facilities for refreshment are there and always there exists an atmosphere of harmony and good humour however pressing the work in hand may be, however timed the arrival.

Present staff are three in number — Miss Jane Dobson, the Association Secretary; Mrs. Carol Clarke and Mrs. Barbara Buchan. Jane (members working at Headquarters dispense with the formality of addressing her as 'Miss Dobson' — surely a sign of their regard and affection for her) joined the staff in 1964 to assist the then Secretary, Mrs. Simpson, continued to work with Mrs. Lack, and finally took over the Secretaryship herself in 1966. That she is capable, efficient to the 'nth' degree and gifted in very many ways is known to all members by now. Perhaps not so well-known, except by those who have had occasion to work in close personal contact with her, are two qualities for which at times many have had reason to commend her. When things have gone wrong she has always remained unruffled; and she has a lively sense of humour. Admirable and important as these attributes are in any secretary, perhaps what one member once said of Jane Dobson sums up very simply, the characteristic in her that there is reason to prize most of all. 'Jane always goes that extra mile to be helpful,' she said. For over ten years now at the nerve centre of Inner Wheel affairs in Great Britain and Ireland, Miss Dobson has given liberally of her time and abilities to being Association Secretary, and in a small way at the 1974 Annual Conference, as a token of gratitude, the Association presented her with a gold wrist watch.

Mrs. Carol Clarke is a member of Inner Wheel with a long, impressive record of service behind her, having been both President and Secretary of the Acton Club, Chairman of No. 13 District, Member of Council and later Association International Service Officer. Back in 1965 she came merely to 'help out' temporarily, but has stayed on, not merely to 'help out' by any means. Visit Headquarters before a Conference and see how inundated with paper-work Mrs. Clarke can be. Visit the office of a morning and Mrs. Clarke is there, sorting out the day's mail. Call in of an afternoon and she is busy lending a hand with any official business requiring urgent attention, yet always she finds the time somehow, kindly to suggest coffee or tea.

The third member of staff at present is also an Inner Wheel member — Mrs. Barbara Buchan, Past President of the New Malden Club (No. 14 District) and at the moment Secretary of it. Since 1975 she has worked at the office, typing, filing, carrying out the hundred and one duties which arise. These three comprise a hard-working, completely compatible team, but not to be forgotten is the debt of gratitude owed by the Association to the many Inner Wheel members of No. 13 District, who happening to live near enough to call in from time to time, voluntarily give valuable assistance.

Those who have held the position of Association Secretary are:

1934/39   Mrs. W. A. Nixon, Manchester (No. 5 District).
1939/49   Mrs. J. H. B. Young, Canterbury (No. 12 District).
1949/62   Miss Elizabeth Eaton (First Paid Secretary).
1962   Miss P. Green.
1962/65   Mrs. E. Simpson.
1965/66   Mrs. L. Lack, Dartford (No. 12 District).
1966/   Miss Jane Dobson.

The wisdom of owning permanent Headquarters is no longer questioned. Admittedly the acquisition of them involved many protracted discussions over a long period of time, but now members can with pride say — 'We have A HOME OF OUR OWN', for it belongs to *them* and as the years go on it is hoped many will feel disposed to call in and sign the Visitors' Book, presented by retiring Members of Council for 1972/73 and feel welcome at 51 Warwick Square, the address to which from all over the country they send their letters of enquiry, their reports and their greetings. Inner Wheel history was made on the day of the purchase of it. Inner Wheel history is being made daily within its walls and will continue to be made successfully there, it is to be hoped, for many years to come.

The Framework

Parts of the Whole and the Parts They Play

The year 1946 was a good vintage year for Inner Wheel in Great Britain and Ireland for it produced a framework within which the organisation has worked happily ever since. Necessary administration had reached proportions which called for the setting up of separate Committees to deal with the different departments of it, and so into being that year came what we now know as the Constitution, Finance, Publications and International (now Overseas Service) Committees. It was not, however, until 1967 that the Chairmen of the Constitution, Publications and Overseas Service Committees were given Executive status. Those then are our Executives of the moment — the Association President; the Association Vice-President; the Association Immediate Past President; the Honorary Treasurer and the Chairmen of the Constitution, Publications and Overseas Service Committees. Also formed in 1946 was a Committee to mastermind the running of the Annual Conference and those concerned in Extension of the movement met together for the first time.

It is neither necessary nor would it be appropriate to spell out here the Rules by which the organisation works. On the other hand, to give a brief run-down on *the parts of the whole and the parts they play* may be justified as being of interest and value to members, particularly the more recently joined who, on hearing of a member holding a specific office such as 'Member of the Association Publications Committee', for example, can be left feeling a trifle bewildered as to what exactly holding such a position entails. Before examining the past histories and present functions of the individual parts, it is necessary, however, to understand how the entire framework is held together.

Within Great Britain and Ireland it is a simple three-tier structure. One Past Association President indeed, is known to have likened it graphically, on her District visits, to the traditional three-tier wedding cake with the Club the basis of all, the District the middle tier and connecting link, and the Association the small top tier. Between Club and Association then the District is the link and the member elected by a District to represent it on the Governing Body is —

The Council Member

Trite it may be to observe that a chain is no stronger than its weakest link, but true it is, and within Inner Wheel one link which certainly must be strong is the Council Member. She is, if you like, the go-between. That may not be a flattering description but it says what it means. She is, however, much more than a mere courier. She has, in fact, to be both councillor and counsellor in the correct meaning of both words.

In the wheel-shaped blue and gold leather book presented to Mrs. Golding in 1937 appear the signatures of the first ever Council Members and Council Members of today and tomorrow may like to know who they were and from whence they came. There was Frances Barnard of Cheltenham; Elsie Clark of Colchester; Gertrude Granville Barker of Wolverhampton; Barbara Anthony of Macclesfield; Bertha Clarkson of Rotherham; Margaret Dawson of Whitley Bay; M. Galliers of Brighton; Blanche Shakerley of Clapham; and the very first Council Meeting was held in September 1934 in Tavistock House, London, by kind permission of R.I.B.I. and there Council continued to meet for many years to come with always, it is recorded, 'the additional blessing of a cup of tea supplied on each occasion'.

Two significant observations were made at the 1951 Annual Assembly with regard to the Member of Council, both of which hold good today. Firstly — that a Council Member must be chosen on merit, *not as a reward for past services*. Secondly — that the responsibilities of Council Members are such that a period of three years' service gives optimum results. Elected democratically then by her District to voice its queries and express its views, the Council Member enjoys the trust placed in her but equally shoulders the great responsibility of faithful inter-communication. Her travelling to, and attendance at Council Meetings is only one side of her work and exacting it can be. Members can take it there are no 'yes' men on an Inner Wheel Council. All participate avidly in every debate, putting forward fearlessly the views invested in them. Seated around the table in order of Districts a Council Member may well find her neighbour holding the opposite opinion on a point, a circumstance she must in no way allow to influence her. Each District is a powerful unit and she its trusted ambassador. The effective discharge of her duty demands too a thorough understanding of the Constitution. Talk, it has been said, which does not end in action is better suppressed altogether, but suppressed talk never is at Inner Wheel Council Meetings which can lead to some very long sessions indeed, but all is given a fair hearing for in matters of moment it is the Council who has the final say as there is precious little use in electing members to this office if they have not the power to make decisions.

Her attendance at Council Meetings, however, a member may very well admit to not being her most demanding hour. The trickiest part of her role, she may with reason feel, is the presentation later to her District of a clear, concise account of what took place there. She must summarise with skill yet devise her report to inform accurately. With time invariably at a premium she may require to be brief. She must manage somehow to interest all her hearers, many of whom may not be Delegates but only interested observers who have simply come for the ride, so to speak, and to enjoy a day out with friends. It can very well happen after all that a hard-working Club member may only be interested in her own thing — in the report of the Overseas Service Chairman, or that of the District Editor. The greater part of the Council Member's report she may dismiss as concerned with issues which seem 'over her head'. Such an observation has been heard. The good Council Member in giving her report will aim at capturing such a member's interest to the point of full involvement.

Writing humorously on that aspect of a Council Member's work, and referring in particular to the possible financial content of it, Dwynwen Plimmer, Council Member for No. 18 District, said in 1963: 'It will take all her piety and wit to convince the District that this or that project which, if adopted, will cost a little more per member per annum, is not a low down attempt to get Clubs to pay off the National Debt!'. And Gertrude Granville Barker, one of the eight original Council Members, then of the Wolverhampton Club, now of the Worthing Club, underlined the importance of the office when in 1957 she wrote — 'A very great deal depends upon the Council Member if the Association is to be served in the best possible way. Much work is done by her and she sacrifices much personal leisure when she assumes the responsibility.'

When problems arise in a District the Council Member is the on-the-spot adviser, the member to turn to. With her knowledge and experience she is a valuable asset in the guiding of new Clubs. She ought immediately to be informed of a new Club's formation. Present at the handing over of any Charter it is she who, in the absence of any Association Officer, who may be a member of the District, conveys the welcome into the world of Inner Wheel.

At present there are twenty-four Council Members representing today's Districts in Great Britain and Ireland. They meet four times a year, three times in London and once immediately after the Annual Assembly. Many-sided and often onerous as this office can be then, and certainly of supreme importance, it affords enormous job-satisfaction. Ask any Council Member!

Law and Order (The Constitution Committee)

Back in 1933 with the prospect of an Association in sight the Drafting Committee which set out to form a Constitution for all, collected together as many Rule Books as were known to exist. Up until this time Clubs in the north had adopted and adapted to their particular requirements the rules used by the Manchester Club whilst Clubs in the south had gone by the rules laid down by the Club of Bexhill, and more or less the same thing happened when early District Committees formed.

An interesting fact emerged from a study of all those Club Rule Books, commented upon by Mrs. Gladys Young at the time in these words: 'The similarity between them was truly remarkable, and so the task of formulating the first Draft was not nearly so difficult as we had thought it might be.'

The first Association Rule Book was printed in 1934. Periodically in the years between then and now, except for the war years when no Conferences were held and so the rules could not be altered, it has been revised, brought up to date, reprinted. In 1947 the Constitution was, in fact, thoroughly overhauled and completely redrafted, but that is not to say the rules laid down in 1934 were radically altered. Changes made were chiefly in the actual wording, not connected with policy. Later the Rule Book became comprehensive, entitled the 'International Inner Wheel Constitution', the first few pages devoted to International Inner Wheel, the remainder to the National By-Laws for the Association in Great Britain and Ireland, this to be used in conjunction with the Inner Wheel Manual which explained the administration. In 1973 the whole was combined into one and in 1976 a further edition of this was published.

The Constitution Committee was set up to watch over the Rules and to advise the Executive Committee and Council on all matters relating to them. This Committee considers requests for advice received from Clubs and Districts on the interpretation of the Rules at any level. It studies any proposals to amend the Rules or any which the Governing Body may contemplate. The Governing Body has never been in favour of continually altering the Rules and perhaps among members there may be some misunderstanding of why it can become necessary. In almost every case alterations arise because a Club or District asks that a point should be clarified and when this is done in one section of the Rule Book it often means corresponding changes have to be made in other sections. When changes are thought to be necessary by Clubs or Districts, the Constitution Committee draft the wording (if wording has not been submitted) and if Council approves of it, it may appear on the Conference Agenda in the name of the Council, but any Club or District has the right to submit a proposal to amend the Rules to the Annual Conference whether the Council approves of it or not, and if the proposal secures a two-thirds majority there, it will be adopted. The power to alter the Rules lies, therefore, only with the members who, through their Voting Delegates at the Conference, decide whether to accept or reject proposals for their amendment.

The membership rules are those which set Inner Wheel apart from other women's organisations and it is proposed changes in these *(which can now only be made at an International Inner Wheel Convention)* which call for the closest study. It is important that a Club's links with its corresponding Rotary Club should not be too tenuous, but members have always been anxious to ensure that widows of Rotarians should be eligible for membership and in fact in recent years the rule regarding them has been relaxed. It is this provision for widows, as well as for the wives of former Rotarians, and the right to transfer, which makes Inner Wheel different from other clubs of Rotary wives.

The rules which govern qualification for office and tenure of it may very well need further alteration in the future, for the lives of women have changed so radically in pattern in the last twenty years and Clubs cannot function if the Rules make it too difficult to obtain officers. Difficulty in finding members to take office, especially in the smaller Clubs, was reflected in the proposal which was passed at the Conference in 1973, to abolish the Rule which made it impossible for a member to hold office in her Club or to serve on the Club's Executive Committee in the year following her service as Immediate Past President. Perhaps, however, the most fundamental change of recent date has been that made in 1974 when the proposal was passed that qualifications earned in one District could be transferable to any other District. Up until then it had normally been necessary for a transferred member to start to earn her District qualifications again when moving to another District, but special dispensations were made for the four new Districts formed in 1972 in order that officers could be found for them.

Also in 1974 it was proposed that the Chairmen of the Association Constitution, Publications and Overseas Service Committees should be nominated by the Districts and elected by the Clubs at the Annual Conference in the same way as are the Association Officers and the Honorary Editor. Previously they had been nominated and elected by the Council, but the proposal that they ought to be more democratically elected because they were entitled to seats on the Association Executive Committee was not opposed by the Governing Body and was passed at that year's Conference.

These then are a few examples of recent changes made to the Constitution, towards it is hoped, smoother running of the organisation. It is felt we can claim now to have arrived at a Constitution which combines authority with flexibility without having departed far from the original intentions, but having so said it is recognised that the biggest room in the world is still the room for improvement and that further changes, not for their own sake, but to meet future needs, may have to be made.

The Constitution Committee is in a special position to appreciate which Rules present difficulties, for it usually examines first of all the problems which are referred to the Association for advice. It is this Committee's particular business to be alive to the need for change and be ready to urge the Governing Body to consider sympathetically any reasonable amendments which Clubs or Districts feel it necessary to propose and it tries at all times to use its influence to ensure that the Rules are a support and guide to Clubs, giving them a sense of belonging to a world-wide organisation which functions on similar basic lines everywhere and is not a straitjacket which hampers the running of any Club.

The Exchequer (The Finance Committee)

Counting the cost sounds such a dismal occupation that members who undertake such work are truly to be regarded not just with admiration but with awe. In fact, the observation has so often been heard within Inner Wheel, 'I couldn't be a Treasurer to save my life. I can't even count my own money!' that the wonder is we have never yet lacked an Association Treasurer, and many highly successful Treasurers have, to boot, not only exhibited financial prowess but have gone on to become highly successful Association Presidents, five of them in all, up to time of writing.

'Whenever a new idea or project is contemplated the very

first question I am asked is invariably — what will it cost?' said Association Treasurer, Mrs. Jessie Casson in 1963. That reflects the cautious approach taken by members to spending. Our Founder would have been pleased to hear it, for from reading her speeches it becomes very clear that it was no part of her intention that Inner Wheel should ever become a costly business for members. That is all very well and highly idealistic, but living in such an ever-changing economic climate as ours has become, and faced with so many unexpected posers, it places upon the shoulders of any Association Treasurer and her Committee a tremendous task.

Attributed to George Bernard Shaw is the remark that, 'If all economists were laid end to end they would not reach a conclusion.' That may be so, but when on investigating and finding present day Inner Wheel financial affairs in as good nick as they are, *we* reach a conclusion — that we can count ourselves lucky in those economist members who have administered our funds.

The belief that when a man is financially insecure, perhaps at the outset of his business career, he more than willingly hands over his earnings to his wife to budget, but when he becomes more affluent he manages them himself, may have in many cases some foundation. Whether or not this circumstance constituted the training ground for any of the female financial wizards who have so adeptly managed our monies throughout the years naturally we know not, but it is only just that their names go on record in this history, for the debt members owe to them is incalculable.

Association Treasurers

Mrs. J. H. B. Young (Canterbury)	1934/44
Mrs. R. H. Tomalin (G. V. Toomey) (Salisbury)	1944/47
Mrs. W. J. Holt (Sutton)	1947/48
Mrs. R. J. Hughes (Uxbridge)	1948/53
Mrs. L. Pickles (Nelson)	1953/55
Mrs. F. M. Leach (Crewe)	1955/59
Mrs. D. Parish (Goole)	1959/63
Mrs. J. Casson (Cheadle & District)	1963/66
Mrs. S. Russell (Bishop Auckland)	1966/69

Mrs. E. F. L. McCready (Plymouth)   1969/72
Mrs. J. Pyke (Birkenhead)   1972/75
Mrs. D. Bailey (Truro)   1975/

Now — having said all that, one might reasonably expect to
read here of the ways and means those Treasurers and the
Finance Committees of the past have employed to keep the
organisation financially solvent; to see figures quoted; balance
sheets examined; but to mention costs of yesterday in any
detail is today quite ludicrous. They have gone so beserk in
recent years comparisons have become meaningless, even
quaint. Decimalisation has in any case changed the entire
picture. To read, for example, that in the mid-twenties the
Club of X paid an annual subscription of one guinea, that
members' badges cost one shilling and sixpence each and that
tea was served at the cost of eight pence per head, that in the
mid-thirties the Club of Y paid only half a crown for afternoon
tea at its monthly meeting, which incidentally consisted of
sandwiches, scones, cakes, biscuits, the lot (evidently counting
calories in those days was of little import), all that may be fun
but purposeless, and even then only fun for senior members
because shortly we will have a generation of members who will
not know all that a mere sixpence could once buy, or indeed
what a half-crown looked like!

And so we do not think it would in any way profit us here to
dwell on actual figures of yesteryear. The accounts rendered
have all been paid. Our heads are well above water. All we
owe is the debt of gratitude to those aforementioned, to those
presently handling our resources and also to every single
member who has contributed her share of thought to matters
financial, for in the Constitution it is stated that the Finance
Committee shall have 'general supervision' of the finances of
the Association, not the entire say. That rests with the member, for on any new proposition for the spending of funds, that
Committee sends its recommendations through the Executive
Committee to the Council.

For those readers who care to glance back down the years
on the reckoning a little, however, we recap briefly here in so
far as to relate that in 1936 it was Mrs. Golding who with

foresight created the first Reserve Fund to be used only in emergency and it was started with the initial sum of £10; that in 1934 the capitation fee really was only sixpence and remained at that figure until 1944 when an increase to one shilling and sixpence became necessary, not surprisingly with the move-ment growing apace and administrative costs likewise. The increase to one shilling and sixpence proved adequate only until 1946. By the end of 1947 the Association showed a deficit of some £200. This circumstance had to be remedied quickly and in place of a further increase in dues an appeal for volun-tary contributions was made. A sum equivalent to two shillings and sixpence per member was received without quibble. It cleared the deficit and provided a working balance for the year.

By this time the Association President was travelling far and wide in the execution of her duties and a very necessary decision had to be taken if the member who undertook to be President was not going to be sadly out of pocket, and so in 1947 it was agreed that her expenses at the Annual Conference and those incurred in her travelling to visit each District once in a year be met by the Association. Then, in the following year with the acquisition of premises and the employment of a secretary naturally there required to be a further rise in the capitation fee and this in 1948 was fixed at five shillings. That no increase had to be made until the year 1962 is surely proof of good housekeeping and, in fact, in 1951 the Association was able to make its first investments. Shrewd and safe ones were chosen — Defence Bonds; the London Trustee Savings Bank and the Post Office. In 1953 the Conference Fares Pool came into force, this to cover the expenses of Delegates in Great Britain and Ireland to the Annual Conference. To begin with the charge was a mere two shillings. By 1962 this had become three shillings and it stands today at thirty pence.

Pointless — and it would be wearisome — to hark back to give a blow by blow account of how costs have climbed since the capitation fee stood at five shillings. Suffice it to say subse-quent rises have all been necessitous and have brought us to today's figure of 85 pence + V.A.T. (1976), an extremely realistic figure when all that has occurred in the intervening years is taken into account — the tremendous upsurge in membership; the fact that we are now a truly international movement; that we own property; have a pension scheme for the staff and substantial securities.

Today's full Finance Committee meet four times in a year, rotas consisting of the Association Treasurer and one member of her Committee being arranged between times to deal with any outstanding matters which call for urgent settlement. For members of the Finance Committee duties permit of no error. They require to be knowledgeable about insurances and investments; to approve to everyone's satisfaction the Draft Balance Sheet presented by the Auditors; to deal with all Fares Pool matters and all expense claim forms for Annual Assemblies and Conferences (this last a formidable task as numbers annually mount); to help in presenting a suggested Budget for the year to come; right down to the relatively simple job of selling coach tickets at the Conference, all this and much more comes within their province and we salute them who, on the ever-shifting sands of monetary standards today, still come forward and somehow manage to keep the organisation in a state of financial equilibrium.

Reviewed here are some of the more recent developments and how we have coped. It was, for example, in the Inner Wheel year 1972/73 that V.A.T. was implemented. This made the Association liable to pay more tax than it had previously done in all its history. It meant that the Association subscription was liable to V.A.T. and anyone who paid the levy for the premises after April 1st would be liable to meet this tax. Whilst some V.A.T. was reclaimable it did not in any respect meet our liability. The rate of the V.A.T. when first introduced was a straight 10% on practically everything.

1973/74 for the first time saw the Annual Conference being costed as a self-supporting event. The only concession made was that if the Association had a one-day Conference — as by its rules it is bound to hold an A.G.M. — then these costs would be borne by the Association. The Association made a contribution based on these calculations. Before this an approximate amount had been contributed by the Association.

It was in this year too, with costs escalating so rapidly, that

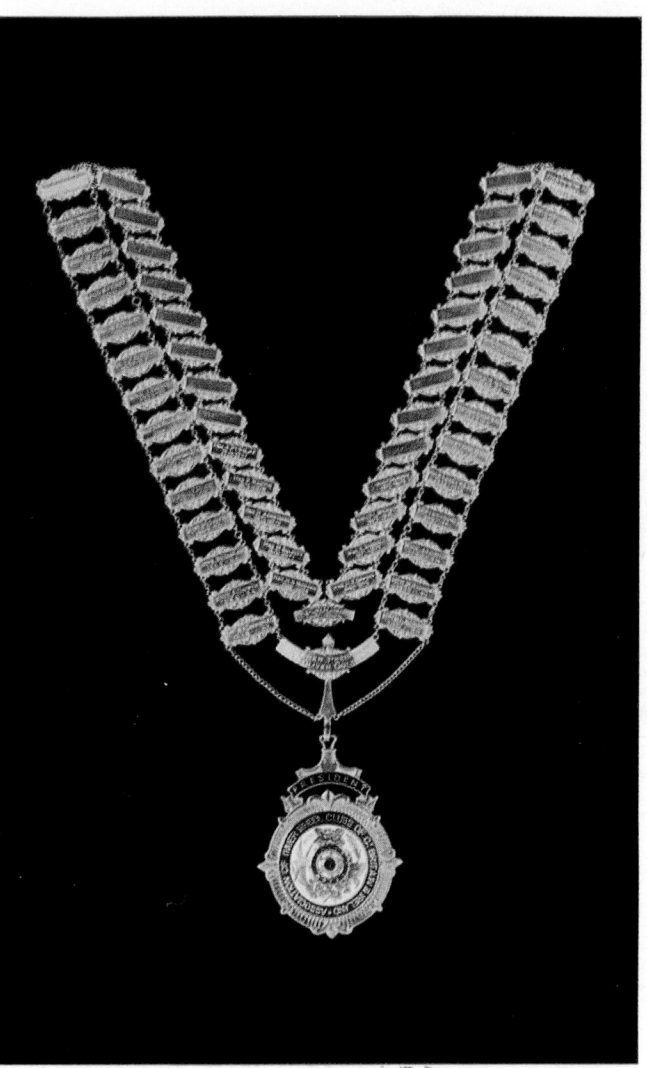

The Association President's Chain of Office.

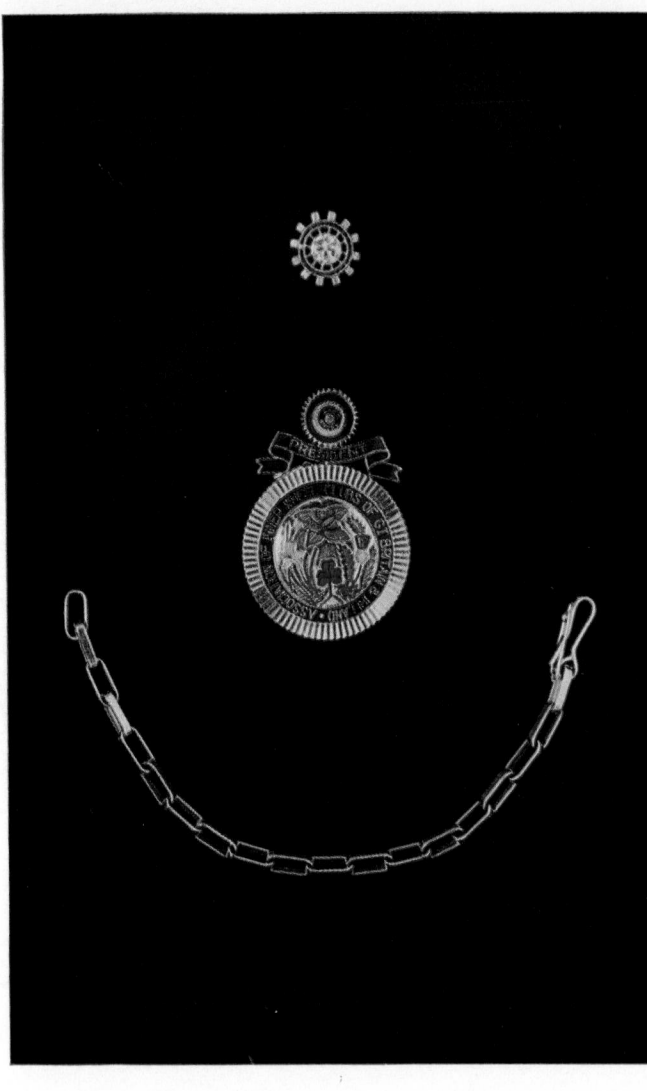

The President's Ring, Badge and Bracelet.

District Chairman's
Badge

Bar

Past District
Chairman's
Badge

District Chairman's
Brooch

throughout the Association the cry went up to practise any economy at all which was practicable. Immediately those Association Committees which were able to do so cut their membership by one ordinary member. This was a much appreciated gesture for it meant the same amount of work being done minus one person, this at a time when the volume of committee work was growing, but they did it, and the Chairmen of Association Committees went a step further to help, by cancelling any meeting which in their opinion was not absolutely necessary.

Now it was that more and more Districts began to travel to the Annual Conference by 'District' coaches. This represented a tremendous saving on the Fares Pool Account, so enabling it to remain constant, this in spite of rising railway costs and more voting Delegates than ever attending the Conference. It was only due in fact to everyone's co-operation that the increase in the capitation fee was held at 21 pence plus V.A.T.

The year 1974/75 brought in changes to the format of the Balance Sheet, which seemed to meet with approval and to make for clarification of accounts for members. It also saw quite a considerable saving being made by the Association Conference Committee, which by the simple expedient of placing Conference Handbooks on seats at the Conference, cut down on postages. In the office too, Miss Dobson, the Association Secretary, agreed to have only one full time member of staff and one part-time member where before there had been two full-time members to give her assistance. To help even further it was agreed that Association Officers who had, for a number of years, been allowed first-class travel would henceforth travel second-class — all except the President. We drew the line there. The President has to be sure of reaching her destination at a given time, otherwise arrangements made in advance for her by others can be thrown out of gear. The strain of her many engagements within a year is considerable and seeing to her comfort en route is the least we can do. And so at the end of that three-year period we emerged able to hand over a year's working balance in hand.

Whilst caring for the present the then Finance Committee took a long, hard look into the future and proposed that the sum of £720 should be invested annually, so that when eventually the lease of 51 Warwick Square falls in, the Association would have funds of approximately £100,000 to play with for new premises, whether leased, rented or bought. This would also cover for the possibility that if ever in the future the Council were to deem it profitable to sell the remainder of the lease on 51 Warwick Square and acquire new premises, they would have the amortisation money to add to the sale price of the lease.

Recent years have witnessed escalating prices on a scale unprecedented in British history and without extremely efficient Association Treasurers and Finance Committees able to cope our own history might have read very differently. For the three most recent holders of the position of Association Treasurer we all must surely feel a particular sympathy — with Mrs. Sybil Russell in office when International Inner Wheel became established who had all the knotty problems concerning foreign currency with which to deal; with Mrs. E. F. L. McCready in office when Decimalisation took over; and with Mrs. J. Pyke to whose lot fell the financial negotiations of the purchase of present Headquarters and the added intricacies of V.A.T., who after all her trials and tribulations, at the end of her spell in office, with infinite good humour simply said: 'Just to see the Committee dispose of approximately one thousand cheques at the Conference Fares Pool payout, with everyone suffering from writer's cramp, having working lunches, breaking off for dinner and returning to work late into the night, checking every individual claim, checking the balance three ways and — eureka! — coming up with everything balanced would have drawn admiration from every member!'.

How fortunate the Association has been that all three of those members took such challenges in their stride and were so well-supported by 'back-room' girls who knew what they were about! Those 'back-room' girls who come forward to serve on the Association Finance Committee have mostly first served an apprenticeship by being Club and District Treasurers, both of which offices demand much homework being done by them before meetings, for they must come prepared to answer searching financial questions which members, as is their right, may put. They can be said 'to come up the hard way' for the management of Club and District Funds is left to them, each Club and District having total control over its own finances. The Association does not dictate and perhaps in that very statement lies the reason for its prospering, or at least one of the main reasons. The only stipulations it makes are that Club subscriptions cover the Association Capitation Fee, the contribution to the Conference Fares Pool and that it is observed that the Inner Wheel Financial year dates from July 1st until June 30th. Dues to the District and to any District Fares Pool have also, of course, to be met, plus the running costs of the Club which vary greatly according to choice of meeting place and amenities, all of which is a purely domestic matter.

The lot then of any Association Treasurer and her Committee, of District Treasurers and Treasurers of Clubs in these days would not appear to be a particularly enviable one, beleaguered as they are by changing values over which they have no control and yet — on meeting members who have served in these capacities one would think it had all been dead easy for them. It could not have been. We conclude that for them the satisfaction far outweighed the chore, when at the end of the day everything added up, as mercifully to date it always has.

The Written Word (The Publications Committee)

Today throughout Great Britain and Ireland each Club (with a membership large enough to warrant production of one) has its own Newsletter; each District its Bulletin; and the Association its Magazine. There now exists in fact a comprehensive network of communication linking us all together in the written word and it is a far cry indeed from the position in 1929 when graciously and encouragingly Mr. Blair-Fish, then the Editor of 'The Rotary Wheel' suggested that a ladies' page might appear in that publication. The offer was, of course, immediately and gratefully taken up.

In 1930 Mrs. Golding accepted the responsibility of editing the page, *editing* but not writing it all, for as is done now for

District Bulletins, Clubs were invited to forward news of their activities. Obviously articles by members to inform and entertain were also sought by Mrs. Golding just as they are by District Editors today, for dipping into two of those old editions of 'The Rotary Wheel' which was to become 'Rotary Service' and then as we know it now, simply 'Rotary', particularly interesting contributions are found by Mrs. P. A. Almy, Founder President of the Torquay Club, No. 17 District. They are highly amusing but at the same time tell of views held, and efforts made, very much akin to those of today. In one entitled 'Tea and Tittle-tattle' she claims, backed by sound, historic authority, that tea and gossip is not, by any means, or ever was, exclusively a woman's indulgence (which makes good hearing for Clubs which cling to the practice of holding their meetings at afternoon-tea-time!). In another she writes in a more serious vein of giving hospitality to young people from overseas, and of how her home in the summer of 1933 was 'a babbilation of strange tongues, as many as four European nationalities being at one time represented at my table.' Such articles as these must have been the answer to the *cris de coeur* of the Founder Editor, for the responsibility of compiling a page worthy of appearing in the official organ of R.I.B.I. must surely have weighed upon her rather heavily.

Nevertheless, Mrs. Golding continued to edit the Ladies' Page until her death, when Mrs. Blair-Fish took over, but only briefly, for on the outbreak of war Mrs. Blair-Fish handed the work over to Mrs. L. W. Barnard who was then the Association President. Courageously Mrs. Barnard accepted this appointment by Council, courageously, for even then presidential duties must have been time-consuming. What is more, Mrs. Barnard continued in that office most successfully right up until 1946.

Long before that, however, she had begun to find it pretty nigh impossible to condense material sent in to her into the confines of one single page. In 1940 'The Rotary Wheel' had become 'Rotary Service'. In 1942 its size was reduced and it appeared only in alternate months due to wartime paper shortage. Plainly it was no longer fair to expect space in it to be devoted to Inner Wheel. Equally plainly what the organisation really required was a publication of its own, and so, permission being granted by Council, Mrs. Barnard set to and began to produce what was to become known as the 'Newsletter'.

For many years the Newsletter was a very modest publication but as finance permitted it grew in size and quality. For a while it was only possible to send one copy out to each Club for the perusal of all of its members, but then in 1950, the Association Editor, who was then Mrs. K. K. Wood, realised an ambition she cherished — a copy became available for every member. In that year too the practice was established whereby Clubs notified, not the Editor, but the Association Secretary of numbers of copies required, which is still the procedure today. To mark the Coronation of Her Majesty Queen Elizabeth in 1953 the Newsletter was given its first Cover in a pretty shade of pale blue. In 1955 the Cover bore a picture of the Presidential Badge in colour. By this time it had become the Association Magazine. The present Cover Design for all but the Annual Conference edition, which generally depicts either a particular scene at the Conference, or prominent personalities of the Inner Wheel Year, although it varies in background colour, was originally the combined work of Past Association Editor Mrs. N. Byles and Miss Mabel Wickham, R.I., a well-known Dorset water-colour artist.

Without any doubt one of the most important years in the development of the Association Magazine was 1946 when several things happened to give it a boost. Up until then all production work had been handled by one person alone — Mrs. Barnard. Time was far overdue for some help to be given and the setting up of the Association Publications Committee provided this. True the Editor retained the right to select for publication contributions she considered news-worthy, just as the Editor retains that right today, but she now had others with whom to discuss lay-out and presentation.

It was in this year too, that Mr. Roger Levy took up the appointment of Editor of 'Rotary'. Ever since R.I.B.I. had sponsored our first venture into print a good and close relationship had existed between both organisations in the written word and for the next thirty years until his retirement in 1975, Mr. Levy was to continue cementing this happy liaison,

and from his extreme kindness, wise counsel and encouragement successive Association Editors, including the writer
herself, benefited greatly.

About this time moreover, it began to be felt that the
Association Editor ought really to be an ex-officio member of
the Council in order that she might be fully conversant with all
Association matters. In 1946 she merely 'sat in' when the
Council considered it advisable. In 1947 she was asked to
attend *all* Council meetings but had no vote. Finally in 1948
she did become an ex-officio member of the Council and her
tenure of office was limited then to five years. Later this was
reduced to three years and still is.

The following members have held the office of Honorary
Association Editor:

1934/39   Mrs. Oliver Golding (Manchester)
1939/46   Mrs. L. W. Barnard (Cheltenham).
1946/51   Mrs. K. K. Wood (Bury).
1951/56   Mrs. R. E. Richardson (Grimsby & Cleethorpes).
1956/61   Mrs. D. J. Proctor (Banbury).
1961/64   Mrs. M. Wyn-Jones (Jones-Pierce) (Aberystwyth).
1964/67   Mrs. N. Byles (Weymouth).
1967/69   Mrs. I. B. Warham (Hendon).
1969/72   Mrs. B. Reed (South Shields).
1972/75   Mrs. D. M. French (St. Andrews).
1975/   Mrs. F. D. B. Morton (Hastings).

There is no doubt that the popularity of the Magazine has
steadily increased with the passage of years. Time was when
members, it seems, were not particularly magazine-minded.
Copies were left behind at Club meetings, but that is not the
case today, at least in the writer's experience, which is surely
indicative of a growing desire to learn about each other and the
Association as a whole. At present the Magazine appears three
times in the year, once in the autumn, once in the spring and
as soon after the Annual Conference as is humanly possible
Clubs receive the special Conference edition and it is to be
hoped that however difficult it may prove to be, publications
will be continued as frequently as is financially viable.

First urged to produce Bulletins of their own in 1946 the

Districts all took up the challenge — some Districts, of course, already had highly successful ones going. There are twenty-four of them now, all of which make absorbing reading. They come in all shapes and sizes dictated by the amount of money available for their production within the District. Some procure advertising matter to offset costs; others not. As a source of information they are invaluable to an Association Editor who reserves the right to 'lift' from them any item she judges might be of interest to readers all over the country. For an Association President these publications are of enormous help, 'filling her in' on a District's geographical background and on projects undertaken for local communities of which she might otherwise never hear.

None of those District Bulletins is simply a bald chronicle of what Clubs are doing, or have in mind to do, although the main content invariably takes the form of reports sent in by the members acting as Club Correspondents. Many articles regional in flavour appear in them and these contributions serve the useful purpose of furthering knowledge and understanding. Often they include tasteful drawings; have well-photographed frontispieces; contain amusing and thought-provoking anecdotes and philosophical quotations chosen for their relevance to the purposes of Inner Wheel. Neither do they all appear simply under the title of 'District Bulletin', but by names both grave and gay — e.g., 'Quinta' (No. 5 District); 'The Twenty Times' (No. 20 District) and for sheer ingenuity and wit surely none can best the title chosen for their news sheet by the Club of Barrow-in-Furness (No. 19 District) in a copy of which in 1951 we read — 'We have asked for, and obtained permission from our Rotarians to call our publication "The Inner Wheelbarrow".'

Both Club Newsletters and District Bulletins then reflect painstaking effort on the part of those members who compile them. Few, if any amongst them are professional writers, yet with considerable skill they manage this vital task of communication. It is not given to everyone the ability to express their thoughts on paper, or to have total recall in order to report selectively what is of import when the event is over but throughout the years has emerged both the willingness and talent to undertake this specialised service, for both specialised and a service it is. The work reaches out to all members including those who through no fault of their own may not be regular meeting attenders, keeping them in touch. It can appeal for aid, or on occasion be instrumental in causing healthy controversy. Above all it forges a strong link between member and Club, Club and District, District and Association.

Holding the office of Club Correspondent, District or Association Editor can be exacting and fraught with pitfalls. It is therefore all the more rewarding when successfully accomplished. For one thing, such members have to be masters of tact. A President or Chairman may hastily correct herself in a speech, but once words go into cold print the impression is pretty nigh indelible, and they must (and generally speaking it is anathema to anyone who likes writing to like arithmetic too!) work to a budget and within recent times what with paper shortages and inflation, it has been truly remarkable how they have cut corners and often the size and number of their pages and have still presented newsworthy editions.

It is so true too that 'purposes of the night fade by daylight'. This is a particular occupational hazard for Correspondents and Editors, and even some Presidents may agree that, inviting Morpheus to exert himself on their behalf and send them to sleep on a night prior to some big day for them, for certain they will be visited instead by the creative muse. Words of wisdom for the speech to be given or the article to be written fairly whizz through the business end of the recumbent form for use next day. It is, of course, on these nights that neither pen nor paper is handy on the bedside table, nor the desire strong enough to procure same. Indeed ere now many scarcely legible hieroglyphics have been scribbled down on paper tissues for this very work, lest the words be lost forever, come the dawn!

The work of the Publications Committee does not consist purely of giving assistance to the Association Editor. Indeed perhaps that is the least demanding of their tasks, for it is they who are responsible for the preparation of all explanatory written matter about the organisation. The choice of wording for the Manual, for all leaflets and pamphlets fall to the lot of

the Chairman and members of this Committee who conscientiously analyse, parse, paraphrase and punctuate, thereafter submitting their final efforts to the Executive Committee
for approval. Usually they have served their apprenticeship as
District Editors and of their number one is a serving Member
of Council.

This Committee's work embraces also the keeping up to
date of all Club histories and District ones, so that, at a flick of
a file any required piece of information can immediately be
found and this is, of course, an ever-growing business. As
each year passes a photographic record of all outstanding
Inner Wheel occasions in Great Britain and Ireland is kept,
one member of the Committee being assigned to the job of
arranging as tastefully as possible the photographs in the
appropriate album.

The only item of current literature which is not actually the
work of this Committee is the Directory. First published in
1937 with just forty pages, by 1951 it contained eighty-eight
larger ones which gave details of five hundred and sixty-three
Clubs in Great Britain and Ireland and fifty-seven Clubs
overseas. Now it is a volume of some hundred and fifty pages.
All details for inclusion in it are still, however, sent to Headquarters in London from Clubs in Great Britain and Ireland
where they are carefully checked by the Association Secretary
before being forwarded to the offices of International Inner
Wheel for final compilation.

One other duty falls upon the shoulders of the Chairman of
the Publications Committee, a rather daunting one. In 1969 it
was decided that she — a copy of all Club Newsletters and
District Bulletins always being sent to her and so being in
possession of all facts relating to Club activities during the
year — she it was who was the appropriate person to present
to the Annual Conference, an omnibus report on work done in
Great Britain and Ireland for causes within Great Britain and
Ireland as distinct from work done for overseas projects. As
can be readily understood this HOME SERVICE REPORT
has been greatly appreciated since its inception by members
attending the Conference. For a Club's project for the year to
have mention in it, albeit anonymously, constitutes for that

Club's members a great thrill, as has been observed by the many covert, impulsive nudges, smiles and happy whispers overheard of 'That was us!'. The report thus serves as a vehicle of appraisal, but cannot be in any way even faintly comprehensive. It has, for one thing, to cover the many forms of service undertaken on World Inner Wheel Day. It has also to incorporate efforts made throughout the entire year and although relatively easy to list the well-publicised among causes to which help is given — the provision of countless Guide Dogs for the Blind; support for the N.S.P.C.C., the R.N.L.I., the R.N.I.D., etc., etc., far less easy is it to discover, compile and include information about personal service given to individuals, and in any event complete anonymity cloaks many of the services rendered as in the case, for example, of a member who may be a 'Samaritan'. Thus it demands that the Chairman of the Publications Committee does her homework assiduously.

Neither are the members of her Committee idle during the Annual Conference. From them live reportage of all events is called for, their copy being turned in to the Association Editor before they leave for home, so that *they* dare not arrive late for, or leave early from, one single session! Moreover, of recent years, they have manned a Bookstall whereat all Inner Wheel publications may be purchased.

Members of the Association Publications Committee are then, in turn, archivists, filing clerks, reporters and salesladies. The Committee has become jocularly and affectionately known as 'Pubs'. To serve on it is to come humbly to know, not only the power of the pen, but to appreciate the many deep and lasting friendships that the written word can promote.

Aid Abroad (The Overseas Service Committee)

Since it was first formed the name of this Committee has twice been changed. Starting as the International Committee in 1946, in 1955 it became the International *Service* Committee, but then, with the establishment of International Inner Wheel, further thought had to be given to its title for the inclusion of the word 'International' in both names was causing confusion and so, as of 1971, it became known as the Overseas Service Committee which clearly indicates its purpose.

Subtly too that purpose has shifted and expanded, for at the very beginning, under the direction of its first Chairman, Mrs. Jessie Park, its programme was confined to 'Urging members to take an interest in international affairs generally; asking Clubs to arrange for at least one speaker in the year to give a talk with an international flavour; encouraging any linguists to take up correspondence with Rotarians' ladies in Europe; and to appointing a Club International Representative who would aim to foster interest in such things'.

In the light of what we know now of the work carried out today throughout Inner Wheel in Great Britain and Ireland in the name of Overseas Service, it is with disbelief that we read in the first records of the Committee that it considered itself to be 'an experimental Committee only which is not looking for spectacular results'.

Response to the aforementioned suggestions was immediate. Ten Districts registered keen interest and within the next two years hospitality for students from overseas was being arranged; assistance was being given with Rotary Exchange Schemes; an escort service for members' children passing through London was in operation; aid was being extended to refugees; and we hear first mention of provision of books for the Ranfurly Library Scheme. Moreover, Overseas Correspondence first embarked upon in 1942 by Association President Mrs. Barnard by 1948 had taken on a new lease of life and contacts by letter on a purely friendship basis, not in any way connected with propaganda for the extension of Inner Wheel, had begun to be numbered in hundreds.

The Committee, it must be said, was extremely fortunate in having Mrs. Jessie Park and Mrs. Elsie Brierley as its first and second Chairmen for both those members were outstandingly strong and forthright personalities. They both could, and did write the most charming but no-nonsense letters to Districts, couched in terms calculated to chivvy members into wielding their pens in the cause of good international relations. Some of the letters they wrote were in questionnaire form, startlingly direct, and they brought results in a big way. After listing seven specific things she wished Club members to do, for example, Mrs. Park ended one letter with the words — 'You may not be able to carry out all my demands, but at least do *something!* And do it right away, thus delighting — Yours sincerely, Jessie Park.' And in 1949, carrying on the good work with like candour, Mrs. Brierley who hailed from the Barry Club, No. 15 District, in sending out a further ten item questionnaire, wrote — 'If your Club can claim to be *internationally minded* you should be able to say "yes" to all these questions.' So neither beat about the bush. They wanted a job done and said so, their aim simply to foster goodwill the world over and what better could they have had? Except to help too, not to restrict their efforts sentimentally to the 'hands across the sea' bit but to create *helping* hands, to give, in fact, AID ABROAD.

In 1961 a Link Scheme was devised, its purpose to develop friendship through correspondence between Districts in Great Britain and Ireland and specified Districts overseas. Two years later a survey of this project showed it to have been a highly successful venture. There had been a great exchange of information by letters, and by messages on tape. Group visits had been organised by Districts; exchange visits between Clubs and individual members had taken place, but the Link-up Scheme ceased to function *officially* in June 1974. There is no doubt whatsoever that in pre-International Inner Wheel days the scheme served as a means of consolidating the movement world-wide, and many are the bonds of friendship which are still today treasured as a result of it, but it had meant the Overseas Service Committee keeping records of the links in operation and of those that had lapsed, finding Clubs willing to be linked, and supplying newly formed Clubs with link Clubs, and due in some part to the failure of Districts and Clubs to report faithfully whether or not correspondence still prospered or had fizzled out, it all became too complex to handle with any degree of accuracy. Clubs are now, therefore, left free to form friendship links with any overseas Club of their own choosing. It is thought better this way.

For a period of time too there was such an office as that of Hospitality Organiser who was appointed annually by Council to serve for three years. An ex-officio member of the Overseas Service Committee, among her many duties was the keeping of a register of all Inner Wheel guests from overseas and all

Inner Wheel members in Great Britain and Ireland prepared to offer accommodation; the arranging of hospitality for any Inner Wheel member left without accommodation in transit due to strikes or travel cancellations; and the escorting of Inner Wheel members' children to and from seaports, airports and stations when requested. This, as travel became more commonplace rapidly developed into a task of gigantic proportion, also one of extremely complicated financial aspects, and although very ably handled for some time, the sheer magnitude of the operation defeated the intention. The practice was therefore scrapped and the office of Hospitality Organiser discontinued.

The Overseas Service Committee of today consists of the Chairman and three others and they meet three times within a year. Of the Chairman it is required that she gives to Conference an annual Report and if the giving of the Home Service Report for the Chairman of the Publications Committee is a difficult assignment, still more difficult perhaps is presenting an account of service given overseas. The giving of it must indeed leave her feeling somewhat unfulfilled for the spectrum of service has grown so wide; the hospitality given knowing no bounds nor boundaries; the help given in cash and kind when national disasters strike wherever the location (always sent through the on-the-spot recognised charities in order that members' contributions reach the correct destination with the minimum delay); the garments sewn, knitted, collected together and despatched; the toys; the books, millions of books now to the Ranfurly Library Scheme which fights illiteracy throughout the world and which organisation now uses in its explanatory literature, we are happy to say, an account of it written in our own Association Magazine in the autumn of 1974. The amount of effort made annually is so fantastic it is quite beyond anyone to 'put over' in a short address.

So the Overseas Service Chairman has one other way in which to convey to members some idea of the volume of work done today. To her all Districts submit reports and these she edits to appear in the Overseas Service Bulletin first published in 1952, and then known as the Overseas Newsletter. By 1957 it had become the Overseas Service Bulletin issued quarterly to District Overseas Service Chairmen only. Nowadays because of ever spiralling cost one issue only per annum is being printed. Always a modest publication it remains so, costing only a few pence, but it *is* available to all members.

There have been in the past other publications connected with Overseas Service which should not go unrecorded. In 1965 the Association produced a book entitled 'Traditional Recipes of the World'. In the foreword to it, Association President Mrs. A. A. Hitching, in recommending it to members as 'providing yet another link in the great chain of international understanding', paid a well-deserved tribute to Mrs. H. E. Hickson who at the time held the office of International Service Officer and had been chiefly responsible for its compilation. It was a fascinating collection of traditional dishes supplied by members all over the world, was spiral-bound in glossy, stain-resistant covers, an asset in any kitchen, and not surprisingly it sold like the proverbial hot cakes. So it was reprinted in 1969, but for some obscure reason initial impact had been lost. This second edition proved to be a slow seller and it was not until after an article had appeared in the Association Magazine calling attention to its merits, that Mrs. D. Cabeldu, then the Chairman of the Publications Committee, was able to declare stocks had been cleared at the Bookstall at the 1973 Conference. It is now out of print.

The 'Dolls of the World' Exhibition held at the 1967 Conference inspired one other publication. Originally the brainchild of the Wollongong Club in Australia, four hundred and eighty-five dolls from nineteen countries all hand-made and dressed by members had been collected together. Already from various exhibitions of them several thousands of pounds had been made for charity in Australia. On show in the Grundy Art Gallery, kindly lent to us by Blackpool Corporation, they attracted over five thousand people and the proceeds were given to the Save the Children Fund. They went then on show up and down the country and again netted a considerable amount for the same charity. And so, subsequently a book entitled 'Cavalcade of Dolls' was produced by the Association, but whether or not seeing dolls illustrated did not have the same appeal as seeing them 'in the flesh', so to speak, the resulting sales were disappointing, incurred a financial loss and all unsold copies were eventually handed over as a gift to the Save the Children Fund.

Members who involve themselves at any level in the work of Overseas Service are at some disadvantage. Seldom do they have the opportunity of seeing the end product of their labours, the causes they support being geographically remote. Such was not, however, the case at the Annual Conference in 1974 when the Overseas Service Chairman, Mrs. H. Barden and her Committee managed to arrange that there was on display in the Horseshoe Promenade of the Winter Gardens at Blackpool, a complete Mobile Clinic which was presented to the Leprosy Mission. Members saw then tangible evidence of their work, in this instance a comparatively passive form of service, for it was simply the result of a corporate collecting of Trading Stamps from the Districts. (This unit, we believe, was later incorporated in the Lord Mayor's procession in London, complete with Inner Wheel Board.)

Distribution of all current literature on all charities which function for aid abroad is undertaken by the Overseas Service Committee in order that Districts and Clubs may have up to the minute information on what is required where. Lists are pathetically and practically endless. Countless names spring to mind unsought, names known to all, all deserving of help. A mere handful only of those to whom throughout the years Inner Wheel in Great Britain and Ireland has sent support of one kind or another can be given here — the Sue Ryder Foundation; the Cheshire Homes; the Flying Doctor Development Service; Unicef; the Red Cross; the Grenfell Mission; War on Want; Mother Teresa; Miriam Dean; Lepra; the Ockenden Venture; and the Royal Commonwealth Society for the Blind, which organisation gratefully in June 1974 devoted an entire issue of their official Newsheet 'Insight' to what Inner Wheel had done for it.

Unfortunately the number of causes do not diminish with the passage of time, and new ones can arise, and so within the Association it is understood that no District Overseas Service Chairman is committed to support a particular charity or charities favoured by her predecessor. She has complete freedom of choice to suggest support for any one of them. In the past to facilitate the work Group meetings were held during the year in York to accommodate the northern Districts and in London for the convenience of the southern ones, but now to economise these have been dispensed with. Most Districts divide into Zones for Overseas Service work with Zone leaders or Area Organisers (either title is permissible). Four Zones are usual and adequate.

At Club level the Overseas Service Organiser is in every sense a master of works. Such members emerge as pretty wonderful people. There is nothing particularly glamorous about the many down-to-earth jobs of assembling layettes, cutting out used postal stamps, sticking trading ones into books, knitting squares which with great expertise are turned into shawls, blankets and bedcovers, and creating out of the merest remnants of material toys, many of which are works of art, and while it is the Club member who with patience and skill actually gets down to those mundane tasks, it is the Club Overseas Service Organiser who cajoles her into doing them, collects the lot and very often staggers under the load to District Overseas Service Rallies there to display them. Visit any District Overseas Service Rally and marvel at the quantity and variety of the results they achieve in order to give comfort to people they will never know, pleasure to children they will never see.

Since International Inner Wheel is now in existence, however, it would seem wise to exercise some caution, highly commendable as the work for overseas causes may be, not to over-exaggerate its importance to the detriment of that devoted to service for causes within Great Britain and Ireland itself. On the other hand it can justifiably be argued that what it all amounts to is — people helping people, wherever they are.

All this then — and those members of the first ever Committee set up for this branch of service within Inner Wheel *'were not looking for spectacular results!'*. Spectacular is a poor word in our book to describe all that is accomplished today to provide AID ABROAD.

The Meeting of the Year (The Conference Committee)

Passing reference has been made to the setting up of a

Conference Committee. By 1946 a separate body of members to handle the arrangements for the Annual Conference was certainly called for. When back in 1928, and the first time in the history of R.I.B.I. Conferences, the ladies were granted the facility of a session exclusively their own, they were privileged to hear speeches made by Mrs. C. A. Mander (Wolverhampton) who was in the chair, and Mrs. Golding. Both made cardinal observations in their addresses.

Mrs. Mander pointed out that anyone whose husband was a *keen* Rotarian must realise that Rotary had got such a hold on him that she had either to take an interest in it or face the fact that she would be left out of a good part of his life. If women refused to be interested it would either have the effect of making their husbands spend still more of their time on it as a protest, or it would damp the keenness and spoil the pleasure they took in it — which view supplies an excellent reason, even if there was no other, for the existence of Inner Wheel.

Mrs. Golding it was who said that the development of acquaintance was continuously being stressed by Rotarians who declared one must go out and meet the other fellow, get his point of view and his ideas and tastes, learn in fact everything about him (borne out in Roget's Thesaurus where 'Rotarian' appears as synonymous with 'a good mixer') which gives a reason that cannot be bettered for the holding of a Conference. 'And why exclude women?' Mrs. Golding asked. Why, indeed!

And so we see attendance rising rapidly after that at the Inner Wheel Business Sessions at R.I.B.I. Conferences — from three hundred and fifty in 1934 to seven hundred in 1936. Gone forever were the days when a small Inner Wheel Enquiry Bureau and an Inner Wheel 'Corner' were features in the Rotary Main Conference Lounge. It now became accepted that the Rotary Conference Committee arranged the meeting place for a full-scale Inner Wheel Business meeting and this held good until 1939. Naturally there were no wartime Conferences and post-war years saw changes. In 1950 Inner Wheel held its first entirely separate Conference. Held at Harrogate it was a big success, but holding an independent Conference like this did have one major snag, that of greater travelling cost for the Rotarian household in which both husband and wife wished to accompany each other to their respective Conferences. Indeed the practice of holding both Conferences in the same town would appear to be the ideal set-up and, in fact, is beginning now to happen more regularly with Blackpool as the venue most favoured meantime. It is, of course, numerically impossible for the Conferences to run concurrently now and the custom has become that of 'ladies first'.

And so to the present, and this Committee which runs the Conference. The Chairman and members of it require above all to be consummate hostesses on a grand scale, the scale every year growing grander for in 1957, to take a year at random, registrations numbered one thousand, nine hundred and sixteen. Ten years later the figure had jumped to three thousand, four hundred. (The 1966 figure had been even higher but it had included Day Registrations which it was decided to discontinue as only local members could really take advantage.) Not the easiest of assignments theirs then, to please that vast number of women when it has been suggested (by menfolk, of course) that it often appears impossible entirely to please one! Yet successive Chairmen have met this challenge with singular success, their only discontent, arising from bitter experience, seeming to be, that complaints of any nature should always be brought to their notice *during* and not after the Conference when there is little they can do.

It is a small team who set out to make a success of *The* Meeting of the Year, the Chairman herself and not more than four others and their duties are multitudinous. Nor can much guidance honestly be given to them from one year to the next for each Conference is subtly different from its predecessor, can pose problems not encountered before and so they must be possessed of great presence of mind in order to make on the spot judgements, adjustments and decisions. You don't have to be a quick thinker to serve on the Conference Committee, in other words, but it helps!

A great deal of spade work is already done before the Committee comes into action at all, a long time before, and mostly by the Association Secretary who does a mass of preliminary investigation and correspondence. Rotary has been consulted;

the venue town selected; its civic authority alerted. The President concerned has planned ahead and has chosen a Deputy Host and Hostess (the Deputy Hostess is a co-opted member of the Committee). She has arranged for them to visit with her what will be Conference Headquarters in order to make personal arrangements and with members of her Executive Committee has chosen those to serve on the Elections Committee. Then and only then, with all the basic machinery set in motion, can begin all the relevant paper work for the Conference Secretary, so gallantly and competently carried out for many years now by Mrs. Carol Clarke. The issuing of all those registration forms; all those badges to be worn for the duration of the Conference and which have changed so many times in type and style in an effort to find the most convenient and popular. Adhesive or pins? The shape? The size? A problem still unresolved to everyone's complete satisfaction. All this constitutes a mammoth task. Little wonder that annually the cry goes up from the office and a plaintive request notice appears in the Association Magazine — 'Please register *early* for the Conference!'.

From the ranks of the Committee there has to emerge a Chief Steward and a Deputy Chief Steward, a Transport Steward and a Flower Steward (for what kind of festival would it be without flowers?). It was in 1947 for the first time that the question of how best to recruit Stewards for general duties arose and a letter was sent out to each District Secretary requesting her to invite six members from her District to help form a rota. Eighty-seven names were received that year of members willing to act in this way and there has never been a shortage since. In 1948 the Committee agreed that red and green lights should be used to limit speeches and a member made responsible for the timing overall, and so gradually the present Conference format emerged.

On the corporate labours of members of the Conference Committee then depends the comfort and well-being of all who attend. They must work in the closest possible contact with the President, see to it that her wishes are carried out and that members of her family who may come to support her are well looked after and yet they must too, be ever mindful of the fact that there are some three thousand others present, many of whom have travelled long distances to be there. So they must be welcoming, polite and helpful, conscious of the little niceties which may make or mar a member's memory of the occasion. The dilemma of a lost handbag . . . A lost husband even (it has been known!). All this and a million and one things besides they are required to deal with competently and willingly.

For their job preparation is all. Obviously they must hold one 'site' meeting to familiarise themselves with all facilities and this is done in the autumn of the previous year. They must organise press coverage and emergency medical aid to be on hand; the distribution of Handbooks; collection bags for the church service; armbands for the Stewards. A veritable plethora of behind-the-scenes and taken-for-granted duties are theirs.

April has become the Conference month which appears to 'fit in' best for everyone and the order of Conference procedure has fallen into a pattern in recent times, a pattern that to improve upon would be difficult, concentrated as it is into two days and yet giving the greatest opportunity possible for — as Association President Kay Martin put it in 1975 — 'Questions to be answered, enthusiasms stimulated, ideas found to refresh and inspire, and for friendships to be renewed, repaired and strengthened.'

Featured at many Conferences have been Exhibitions held in aid of various causes. Holding any such calls for quick organisation, the question of finding a suitable site and the setting out of exhibits when at the last moment they arrive. Not easy, but there is no doubt they all have been extremely attractive and successful. In 1966 the 'Dolls of the World' Exhibition was held, the proceeds of which went to the Save The Children Fund; in 1967 an Exhibition of Paintings by members helped the Leprosy Mission. Proceeds from an Embroidery Exhibition in 1968 were sent to the Royal National Institute for the Deaf and from the Exhibition of Knitting in 1969 and one of Soft Toys in 1972 proceeds were given to individual Club Charities.

No account of past and present Annual Conferences would be complete which omitted mention of the Inner Wheel Golf

Trophy and the contest for it. The custom of holding this competition did not emanate from Scotland as did the game itself, but it did originate in the north, in No. 3 District. In a 1951 Rotary Conference Daily Bulletin there is mention of a Golf Competition for ladies, whether or not they were Inner Wheel members, played at St. Annes for the 'Mrs. Hugh Galloway' Trophy. (Rotarian Hugh Galloway of Newcastle was a Past President of R.I.B.I.) Then in 1955 to commemorate her Presidential year, Mrs. Joan Egner, also of No. 3 District, presented to the Association the Inner Wheel Golf Trophy which is competed for today. In 1976 for the first time a competition of nine holes only was also played, Mrs. Egner generously donating the prize and, incidentally, ending up by winning it! This prize, Mrs. Egner has delicately put it, is for 'Veterans' only. Over several years now it has been Mrs. Isabel McKnight of the Sale Club, No. 5 District who has very successfully carried out all the organisation of the Golf Tournament.

Readers of the Conference edition of the Association Magazine which endeavours to convey a blow by blow word picture of all that happens at the Conference will be by now familiar with the routine — the benediction of the ecumenical church service, very often now beautifully contributed to by a choir recruited from members; the opening Conference Session; the evening entertainment generously given by the Civic Authorities who always give graciously so many other perks, including the cute little freedom vouchers entitling members to, amongst other things, the luxury of free deck chairs. *In April!* (No one has as yet been seen availing themselves of this amenity, however tempting. The time factor forbids!) The next day's Annual General Meeting which hopefully is completed in the morning but has been known to continue well into the afternoon, then leads to the Presidential Address and on the second and last evening together members foregather at the President's Evening, her hour of glory, when she endeavours to meet and greet as many Club Presidents and members as is humanly possible — and for the arranging of every session of it all, hard at work still are — who else, but the members of the Conference Committee.

Those are the Committees then which together with the members who work for the Extension of the movement form the basic structure, and for the solidarity of that structure plainly the need for an annual get-together of Officers from all of the Districts with the Association President and members of the Executive Committee is a necessity.

The Briefing

THE establishment of an Annual Assembly came about gradually. Prior to 1939 District Chairmen and District Secretaries met during R.I.B.I. Conferences, exchanged views and discussed problems. As the years went on, however, it became evident that other District officials should have the opportunity and benefit of meeting, if not for actual instruction, at least for a BRIEFING on what was expected of them. Separate meetings for District Correspondents (now District Editors) with the Association Editor began to take place; similarly meetings of Extension Chairmen. These meetings were irregular, all held in London at various venues and were simply of one day's duration, which could not have been all that satisfactory, and so in 1947 it was agreed that a meeting be held of District Chairmen, District Secretaries, District Editors and District Extension Chairmen all together in early July of that year, this to be held in the Berkeley Rooms of Zeeta's Restaurant, Putney.

This address was to become familiar to all in the following years for it became the scene of a great many meetings, always growing in importance as more and more District Officers were invited to attend. In 1948 District Treasurers first attended. In 1950 International (Overseas Service) Chairmen were included and finally it was decreed that Council Members should be present. For the record 'Zeeta's' no longer exists. Initially a large Confectioners it then became a high-class Restaurant and Ballroom. Today the concern is divided up, one part a grocery store; another a wine shop and on the ground floor a fashion salon.

Now into being then had become a corporate Annual Assembly for all District Officers and in 1951 — it was the year of the Festival of Britain and it was thought that finding accommodation for all Officers might prove difficult in London — a Conference Centre was booked for a period of two days. This was High Leigh, Hoddesdon, Herts., a name well known now throughout the organisation. Mrs. R. E. Richardson, who was then the Association Editor, wrote of the first occasion there — 'Imagine a perfect summer evening. The shafts of golden sunlight reflected on the still waters of a lake, fringed with countless rhododendrons, a contrast to the little dark paths which meander through the trees. Pre-eminent is "High Leigh", a stately mansion of architectural beauty and dignity. Such was the setting as District Officers were welcomed by the incoming President (Mrs. W. E. Rice). Many felt that the unrivalled natural opportunities for new friendships thereby afforded, more than compensated for the possible attractions of city hotels'.

Here then the Annual Assembly has been held successfully ever since, on or about July 1st each year. The Centre has been adequate up to now (1976) but because of the increase in the number of Districts, difficulty in housing all Officers is now beginning to be felt, the difficulty for the moment being resolved by one group of Officers meeting instead at Association Headquarters, its 'leader' travelling afterwards from London out to High Leigh to present her Report to the open Assembly.

The new incoming officer arrives here in search of guidance. Her knowledge of the duties which lie before her is confined at this point to observance of what her predecessor has done — and if her predecessor has done an outstandingly good job she may well be all the more apprehensive of following her — *but* she is armed, or should be, with whatever information her predecessor has chosen to give her. Now, on this planet man is unique in that only man can pass on his acquired knowledge and experience. If that smacks of sermonising it is not intended so, but offered rather as a thought for Officers demitting office and 'handing over'. It is of paramount importance and only kind to the 'new girl' to deliver to her a full dossier.

Reactions of Officers attending the Assembly for the first time have been reported many times, and all admit to the fact that attendance there has come as something of an eye-opener

Lapel Badge   Honorary Member's
                                    Bar

Club Member's   Secretary's Bar
    Badge

Name Bar for Club
President's Collar

Club President's
Badge

Past President's
Badge

to them, for it is only then many realise the amount of preparation which is necessary for smooth continuity into a new Inner Wheel year. The two-day programme is a full one. Each Group is 'taken' by the appropriate Association Officer. The value of personal contact with that Officer is inestimable, as is meeting and talking with those from other Districts with the same job in hand.

Any incoming Officer then returns to her District, clear in her mind as to her duties, vastly more confident than when she arrived and always greatly encouraged by the friendships she has made, and so she is capable of giving, and eager to pass on a similar briefing to all Club Officers. In this way it has become customary to hold a one-day District Assembly, this as early as is practicable in the Inner Wheel year.

The Annual Assembly at High Leigh has always been a strictly business-like affair. It is no social occasion and yet it would be quite unfair to put it down in history as never having had its lighter moments. It invariably has, for a light entertainment is provided on the last evening, in the main the responsibility of the District to which the incoming Association President belongs, although all Districts are invited to, and often do give of their talents, to the surprised delight of their fellow members who up until then have only seen them applying themselves to serious Inner Wheel affairs. And here mention must be made in the passing of the contribution to the Assembly, annually made by the local Club of Hoddesdon (No. 9 District) which thoughtfully has provided for many years now all manner of niceties to make enjoyable for everyone their attendance at the Annual Assembly.

Peeps into the Inner Wheel Diary

THE Inner Wheel year runs from July 1st until June 30th. In most Clubs throughout Great Britain and Ireland, however, July and August are looked upon as holiday months, so that the first Club meetings of the year are the September ones. Then the honeymoon is over and activities begin in earnest.

Membership which can be of three kinds, Active, Honoured and Honorary (the Manual explains the categories fully) entitles attendance at Club Meetings, the member's own Club or any other *throughout the world*. Any Club member has the right also to attend District meetings and where a Fares Pool exists Club Delegates are paid, two from a Club of up to fifty members, three from a Club having more than fifty Active members including Honoured Active members. (Honorary members do not count in this total.) Many and various are the other 'dates' which members can have with their friends in Inner Wheel, dates which they can nowadays enter in attractive blue Inner Wheel Diaries obtainable from Association Headquarters. There are Inter-Club Luncheons and Club Birthday Parties, District Rallies, District Overseas Service Rallies and Charter Presentations, all these generally by ticket and choice.

And here perhaps is the appropriate place for a brief digression. Most members within a Club eventually come to know each other on first name terms which is only natural and as it should be, but in Club Newsletters, District Bulletins and Minutes which may, and in some cases indeed, *ought* to be sent to others — e.g., District Bulletins to the Association Editor — the use of christian names *only* has been viewed by some with consternation, for 'President Jean' or 'Secretary Margaret' often means nothing to the recipient. The practice can also be somewhat off-putting for first time visiting members to a Club meeting, or for a member present at her first District meeting. It did, in fact, prompt one member to write complainingly after attending a District meeting at which she had found herself at a complete loss — 'Surely it is over-doing the informality!'. Discretion is perhaps the better part of friendship here.

This is surely where BADGES play their part. From the earliest days we have had badges and have worn them with pride, badges showing our name, our Club, any office held and offices held in the past. In some Clubs it is the practice to 'fine' those forgetful of wearing them, a nominal few pence, pro-ceeds going into a fund used for the provision of flowers for any ailing member and it is known that providently in one Club at least, monies so gathered are put towards de-fraying the ever-rising cost of heating a rather chilly meeting room. Of course, it is purely a domestic matter, but to pur-chase a badge and not to wear it would seem to be a meaning-less exercise.

The wearing of the tiny lapel badge is to be highly com-mended. On the eye encountering this miniature symbol of membership on another's coat when travelling, at once some-thing of curiosity to know her stirs, the tentative smile begins, hopeful of a reciprocating one, and before any rapport is established, tacitly another member becomes a friend because understanding of each other's ideals already exists. So you think this is not history? But, of course, it is, for each single meeting, member with member, even if it should turn out to be a once-in-a-lifetime one, that is what is making our history day by day, building and strengthening it. That this small emblem is recognised as representative of service, and has been for some time now, is well illustrated in the story of the day when Mrs. D. Parish, the Association Treasurer in 1959/63, was approached by a fellow traveller, the wife of a serviceman serving abroad. It transpired the young woman had a problem, that of having to rejoin her husband overseas, leaving a young daughter alone in a school in Yorkshire. As a result of that chance meeting the local Inner Wheel Club 'adopted' the little girl and by correspondence kept the anxious parents assured of their daughter's welfare.

And now, while on the subject of membership and all it means, let us explode some myths together . . .

In some mysterious way, in some quarters, membership of Inner Wheel has become connected with affluence, yes, even today! This is simply not the case — nor indeed would it have to be in many Rotary and Inner Wheel households. Membership embraces all walks of life, the wife of the butcher, the baker, the lawyer and doctor. It is the degree of *caring*, not of wealth, which brings membership which is not to imply that non-Rotarian and non-Inner Wheel butchers and bakers are not caring people. Stating the obvious? Not at all. Clarifying rather what is Inner Wheel and underlining what Mrs. Golding all those years ago was wont to say 'that an Inner Wheel meeting should not be felt to be a pull on the purse'.

Two other misconceptions are by now effectively quashed. Scotched forever is the image of the middle-aged matron, extravagantly behatted, quaffing tea and wolfing cream buns mid-afternoon. The present day Inner Wheel member is much more likely to attend a meeting casually attired, minus any hat, sporting a business-like trouser suit and eschewing all confections with her sugarless tea in order with comfort to 'get into' her functional outfit. Likewise the label 'do-gooder' has died a natural death, although why the term should be synonymous with condescension is a poser, for surely it means 'of good intention' and what is wrong with that? Members of Inner Wheel have never in any way merited the use of the word. The vast amounts which have been raised for charities, local and nationwide, would certainly make many eyebrows climb, but the organisation does not advertise them, not being a money-making one in the first place. Sums raised may appear in the local press out of fairness to local support — indeed should be — and many corporate efforts because of the magnitude of results have been received by people of renown, even acknowledged by royalty, but it is an unwritten law that totals reached do not appear in the news from Clubs for District publication, for what to some may constitute small beer may after all appear to others a grand total, and so relationships on that score are kept sweet within the Association.

Finally, the remark 'There is nothing so past as a Past

President!' which has been heard within Inner Wheel, and no doubt within other organisations, has now been proved to be a pure fiction, and ought to be amended in everyone's book to read — 'There is nothing so *valuable* as a Past President', for is it not she who has made history? Isn't that what this book is all about?

So she is no longer in the chair. She may even have convinced herself she has had her day. Nothing is further from reality. She has a place in the future of her Club, and her role is now a delicate one, that of guide and mentor. Asked as she will be for advice and help this she must give, calling upon her experience, but at the same time exerting tact and restraint so that whatever she says can never be called interference. Members present at the Annual Conference in 1973 will surely agree with this view when they recall the great and wise counsel given on the spot, quite voluntarily and unrehearsed, by Past Association Presidents when the question of the purchase of present Headquarters was being at one point very actively and somewhat hotly debated. It was then with modesty but forthrightness too, that they came forward and proclaimed that, in their time, they wished that they had been possessed of sufficient courage and foresight to acquire property. How sensible were their remarks and how they were heeded and acclaimed! Yet they very well could have just sat there, but they did not. They *contributed*.

Now it is held by many that womenfolk are possessed of a sharper critical faculty, particularly of each other, than menfolk. It is, therefore, all the more extraordinary that, on going through the bare bones of the history of Inner Wheel, there are so few of real contention, but it is truly the case. Working closely together at all levels members appear to show uncommon good sense and are too occupied with the job in hand to indulge in petty squabbling. Not that Inner Wheel holds any mystique about it in creating good relations. It would be a nonsense to suggest such a thing. All members do not 'take to' each other as limpets to rock, but the basic contributory factors to the bonhomie which exists are many. There are, for example, no classifications for membership, for as R.I. President Bill Carter pointed out in his address to the Inner Wheel

Conference in 1974: 'There would be no classification wide enough to embrace the occupation of *housewife*.' How true! And, as in Rotary, there are no barriers to membership in race, creed, religion or politics. Neither is there any age limit, a feature of some importance.

The writer, for instance, was in her early twenties when she joined her first Club, found mother figures among the senior members and benefited from their knowledge and wisdom (which is not the same thing!). Equally she met up with others of her own generation with whom to identify, and share both the pleasures and problems of membership, and many real problems there were, before the advent of nursery schools, convenience foods and mechanical home aids. Regular attendance at meetings could be hard to maintain as initially afternoon meetings were the order of the day. In recent years this has to some extent solved itself, many Clubs, especially new ones electing to meet of an evening. To change to this practice, however, it must be said, can hold the attendant danger of losing senior members, particularly in older Clubs, for not unnaturally the idea of turning out to attend meetings in an evening does not appeal to them so strongly.

No newly-joined member is ever permitted to feel herself 'a new girl'. From the day of her first meeting she is given (or ideally should be) some responsibility, for 'there are no rights without corresponding obligations', which words, or some such, are incorporated in her initial welcome. One other phrase concerning membership which is of supreme importance is that which says — 'Once an Inner Wheel Member, always an Inner Wheel Member'. Provided there has been *no break in the payment of her dues,* membership is a lifetime affair. The demise of a Rotarian husband does not mean Inner Wheel membership comes to an end. Quite a number of Association Presidents have been the widows of Rotarians.

Participation is the keyword for the full enjoyment of membership. Sitting on the sidelines watching the action is no fun compared with the sense of fulfilment experienced from a tenure of office, for however short a time and however much a member may doubt the value of the contribution she can make. Whatever she does well — and there must be something

— there is need for that ability somewhere in the organisation. The phrase — 'Doing your own thing' some may dismiss lightly as merely trendy vernacular but it is no new concept. Back in the fifteenth century, in his poem 'Truth' Chaucer advised: 'Suffice thine owene thing though it be small'.

Opportunities *sans pareil* to make friendships at a distance, not necessarily international ones, are afforded by membership. With great thought the Association President in 1969, Mrs. H. E. Offord, and her Executive Committee instituted a District Link Scheme within Great Britain and Ireland. Today those Links flourish, particularly at Annual Conferences when coffee evenings and tea parties organised by the Districts linked are fitted in to the tight two-day Conference schedule and Chairmen of linked Districts are only too happy to be invited and travel to each other's District Rallies. A one hundred per cent active link, Club with Club would be ideal. Somewhat surprisingly there has, however, been found resistence to this. 'Why link us at such a distance with such and such a Club?' the cry has been heard, but in the great majority of cases it has become rather a pleasant exercise for members to try finding their 'opposite numbers' at Conferences to exchange greetings, views and ideas.

These then are some of the privileges of membership, and the greatest entitlement of all it could be said is attendance at the Annual Conference. This is an experience, the one and only way to come to realise the magnitude of the movement. It is a 'must' for any member who takes her membership seriously to attend at least one Conference. It is a fairly safe bet that she will come to another and yet another. This is where the action is. We know from looking at the work of the Conference Committee a little of the back-stage story. From the member's point of view it all looks rather different and a brief step-by-step résumé of a typical Conference of today may resolve a few question marks.

The member will arrive in the Conference town on the Monday most likely, very early that day, or perhaps on the Sunday, if she is entering for the Golf Tournament. She will find her accommodation, find the hotel where the Conference

Headquarters office is housed, find where she is expected to vote if she is a Delegate — and in all fairness any voting should be done *as soon as is practicable*. Without doubt by this time she will have encountered friends and by nightfall that first day will find herself involved in a link District get-together.

Next morning she will attend the Church Service at which of recent years the collection for a charity of the President's choosing has incredibly come near to reaching a four-figure total. In the afternoon she will be present at the first Conference Session which most years is graced by the presence of the President of Rotary International or the President of R.I.B.I., or both, who bravely come to address the gigantic practically all-female audience — although always it has been noted there are a number of interested Rotarians present to lend them moral support! If her world-wide commitments allow the President of International Inner Wheel will be there and the President of the National Association of Ladies' Circles, that vigorous, youthful Association with aims and objects so similar to our own. Often too a special Guest Speaker has come at the President's invitation. Finally at the end of the day the member will be privileged to attend a Concert given by the civic authorities.

On the Wednesday morning at the Annual General Meeting she will see the Business carried through. Now, it has been humorously suggested that any Conference can be defined as 'a gathering of important people who singly can do nothing, but together can decide that nothing can be done', but in the annals of Inner Wheel this has not been so. None have been purely grand scale social occasions. All have accomplished something towards betterment in handling Inner Wheel internal affairs and some have, in General Resolution form, made clear members' views on matters of national concern and subsequently these have been conveyed to the appropriate authorities. As the Association grows in size, greater stress than ever before is being placed on this aspect. Indeed Association President Mrs. Joan Pyke, in her address to the Annual Assembly in 1976, made a strong appeal to members to use their influence more in the realm of public affairs than has been done in the past, and to implement at Club level any resolutions passed at the Annual Conference, for the voice of Inner Wheel, the voice of some thirty-two thousand women in these islands should, it is held, not go unheard in our society.

Let any who level criticism of what has or has not happened of value at past Conferences here reflect on two things. Where has lain the fault? The answer, if the accusation has any truth in it, would lie in member apathy. And how, if successive Annual Conferences have not accomplished all they might have done, how then can the growing strength of the movement be explained?

Later that same day with the Business despatched the member will hear the President's address, and if any item of Conference procedure can be singled out as a highlight, this is it, for looking back through Presidential addresses, all the long way back right up to the present, it is remarkable how interestingly varied presidential observations have been on what is after all the same theme. So little repetition when repetition could have been the easy way out!

The President's Reception and Party in the evening is the grand finale, when at last even the President herself may relax (except to remember to remove any rings she may be wearing if she is not to be incapacitated by a painful right hand next day after all the congratulatory handshaking!). Colourful and gay, this auspicious occasion is something to remember for a lifetime. It is *the* outstanding evening in the Inner Wheel year for friendship, albeit tinged with some emotion and nostalgia for members of long standing, for it is a climax, marking not quite but nearly, the passage of another Inner Wheel year, the era of yet another President.

As part of the entertainment offered to members who attended the Conference in 1951 a whist-drive was held in the Headquarters hotel — *a whist-drive!* Such a thing cannot be imagined nor would be feasible today and yet such is the quality of the friendship shown, the increase in attendance has in no way meant that the Conference has become impersonal. Very personal indeed are some of the contacts made, as in the case of one international relationship which was triggered off by the merest chance and by, of all things, a member's migraine.

At the President's Party she found the music too distressingly rumbustious for her. She sneaked back guiltily to her hotel, only to encounter seated in the deserted foyer of it, one other solitary female, also wearing a Conference Badge, who looked up to murmur 'Migraine. I just couldn't make the President's evening and feel so thwarted!' 'Two fellow sufferers out of over three thousand here. How remarkable we found each other!' was the feeling reply. It is not known if, over the subsequently shared cup of tea the migraines of the evening vanished, or if either sufferer found a remedy. What is known is that those two, although a continent separates their homes, became firm friends and have corresponded ever since. A whimsical anecdote perhaps, but an example of the happy, history-making little incidents of which there must be very many and which naturally go unrecorded but enrich the lives of members everywhere.

If yesterday R.I.B.I. Conferences were stepping stones to Inner Wheel formation — and they were — the Annual Conferences are milestones in the life of the Association today.

TOMORROW

Past Presidents of the Association

1934–1936	Mrs. Oliver Golding (Manchester)
1936–1937	Mrs. W. A. Shakerley (Clapham)
1937–1938	Mrs. B. Jennings (Mrs. Anthony) (Macclesfield)
1938–1939	Mrs. E. A. Gower (Putney)
1939–1942	Mrs. L. W. Barnard (Cheltenham)
1942–1944	Mrs. E. M. Billingham (Ramsgate)
1944–1946	Mrs. H. Laycock (Mrs. Lewis) (Scunthorpe)
1946–1947	Mrs. H. H. Coote (Wimbledon)
1947–1948	Mrs. H. Barnacle (Coventry)
1948–1949	Mrs. J. E. Park (South Shields)
1949–1950	Mrs. M. Gaskell (Rossendale)
1950–1951	Mrs. T. H. Gameson (Walsall)
1951–1952	Mrs. W. E. Rice (Margate)
1952–1953	Mrs. E. H. McKellen Wild (Conway)
1953–1954	Mrs. K. K. Wood (Bury)
1954–1955	Mrs. R. J. Hughes (Uxbridge)
1955–1956	Mrs. F. G. Egner (North Shields)
1956–1957	Mrs. V. P. Barrand (Bristol)
1957–1958	Mrs. R. E. Richardson (Grimsby & Cleethorpes)
1958–1959	Mrs. W. E. Homer (Dudley)
1959–1960	Mrs. F. M. Leach (Crewe)
1960–1961	Mrs. D. M. Parry (Pontypridd)
1961–1962	Mrs. L. N. Darbyshire (Ripley)
1962–1963	Mrs. J. G. Cheer-Moody (St. Marylebone)
1963–1964	Mrs. M. Foster (Brighouse)
1964–1965	Mrs. A. A. Hitching (Bristol)
1965–1966	Mrs. D. M. Weightman (Purley)
1966–1967	Mrs. P. Ponting (Andover)
1967–1968	Mrs. C. W. N. Sharp (Reading)
1968–1969	Mrs. H. E. Hickson (Castleford)
1969–1970	Mrs. H. E. Offord (Redhill)
1970–1971	Mrs. M. Bulpitt (Birmingham)
1971–1972	Mrs. S. Russell (Bishop Auckland)
1972–1973	Mrs. H. Armstrong (Coleraine)
1973–1974	Mrs. E. F. L. McCready (Plymouth)
1974–1975	Mrs. L. H. Martin (Bognor Regis)
1975–1976	Mrs. C. N. Moon (Shepton Mallet)
1976–1977	Mrs. J. Pyke (Birkenhead)

Tomorrow . . .

IT may seem odd to preface a chapter entitled 'Tomorrow' by giving a chronological list of the Presidents who have served the Association in the past, but back in the beginning, the promise was given that this was to be a history with a difference, and is the list so out of place on reflection? Is it not, after all, upon the legacy those members have left behind them that the future of Inner Wheel has to be built?

Examine the list and note how those members have hailed from Clubs large and small and most areas. It is true a few minority group regions have not yet had the opportunity of supplying an Association President, but the time will come, may even have arrived, before this history is complete.

At no time has the Association lacked leadership and all Presidents have followed closely in the steps of the Founder, adhering to the principles she outlined. It is worthy of note too, how despite the many social changes which have come about, and could so easily have caused members themselves to deviate from certain avenues of service, they have remained loyal to them — the advent of the National Health Service, for example. Yet still today even as in Mrs. Golding's time, all over the country inestimable service is given in hospitals.

Each President in turn has displayed great devotion to her duties. Every single one of them has had a different approach to the job. None has been a mere figure-head. It cannot be claimed that any one of them came to the office gifted with Churchillian oratory, yet members have listened and learned when they spoke. Is there then a charisma about such members which marks them down as leaders from the outset? If so, it is plain they themselves have been unaware of it, for talk to any one of them and it will emerge that none even in their wildest dreams imagined holding such a position. Nor have any set out with the deliberate intention of becoming President. This would not work in any event, for lobbying for any office whatsoever has always been strictly taboo.

A Club member may meet an Association President only once and then but briefly at a District Rally, or may only see her from afar presiding at the Annual Conference. Consequently it can at times be difficult for her to equate with the beautifully groomed platform personality, wearing the delectable Conference hat (not an idle conceit this, it must be said, but rather a compliment to her fellow members in that she has chosen to give them something attractive to gaze upon) with the woman herself. Easy to forget she runs a home and quite often a business as well, looks after a busy Rotarian husband, cares for a family and carries out daily all the unglamorous domestic duties like any other member. She may *appear* a woman apart. She is nothing of the sort, simply an *ordinary* member (that unfortunate description for which a better has yet to be found).

She took office whenever she was asked, as Mrs. Golding urged, for history was never made by those who put off until tomorrow, or have been afraid of responsibility, or have fought shy of the limelight which can result. It also has to be borne in mind that she by no means confines herself to giving service for 'her' year only. The duties which devolve upon a Vice-President and an Immediate Past President are numerous. Handled with enormous competence the Presidency then has undoubtedly been but competence is far from all. Among other qualities, not so easily demonstrated in the position, but common to all, for looking back it is impossible to remember one lacking it, has been a sense of humour, probably one of the greatest personal assets in today's world, when so many happenings appear at first sight catastrophic, but can, at the drop of a light-hearted remark, fall immediately into perspective.

This ability to laugh things into correct order of importance was illustrated to perfection by the Association President (who out of delicacy will remain anonymous but would be the first to smile if she *were* to be mentioned by name) who when asked to reminisce on 'her' year, confided that, out of a number of months of being President, she had managed to spend only three days in her own home, three nights in her own bed, and that she had discovered a cobweb — yes, a cobweb on the landing in her house, and how at first sight of it her housewifely instincts had been outraged. 'But you know,' she said. 'I became quite fond of it. I couldn't reach it and looking at it as closely as I could, I saw the wonder of it, how each strand depended one upon the other, how, in fact, just like Inner Wheel it was stretching out.' Over-fanciful? Not a bit of it. She had become, somewhat to her own surprise, a carefree, out-going personality, no longer worried by trivial things.

So — from where will they come, the Presidents of the future? From which Club? Yours or mine? It is anyone's guess and an excitement upon which to speculate, for it has been said not once but many times, and is still worth repeating, *every* member is a potential President.

And right across the board too those who will form the Secretariat of tomorrow will be of enormous importance. The future would look bleak indeed if members willing to undertake the duties of Club and District Secretaries were not to emerge from the ranks. Some are known to be fearful of assuming this office. Why? It has not mattered in the past if such members were *trained* secretaries. Very few in fact have been. Fluency in shorthand and the number of words typed per minute are of little import. Much more to the point is it that they are prepared to be true help-meets, willing Girl Fridays of the outfit, availability probably their most important role, their reward lying in the knowledge that there is always considerable consternation in the Club if they are not there, if only to give the apologies! And, of course, the complimentary bonus of being always bracketed with the President in such phrases as — 'The President and the Secretary are our Delegates' and 'The President and the Secretary represented us'.

A three-year stint as Club or District Secretary is eminently desirable. There is too much to digest in less time than that. Even Miss Elizabeth Eaton, the first *professional* Secretary employed by the Association in her first report to the Conference in 1950, had this to say — 'My first twelve months have been spent in *learning* about the work, making mistakes and profiting by them. With twelve months' experience to draw on, I now hope to be a much more competent servant to the Association'.

The injunction 'Write to the Secretary' may have an ominous ring about it, for it suggests there is doubt, dissatisfaction or at worst real trouble brewing, but at the risk of being accused of stating the obvious, it is sound advice. That is what secretaries are for, to write and be written to. They form a members' advice bureau, yet members of Inner Wheel can be as guilty as anyone of registering complaints in the wrong way, complaining amongst themselves, complaining too late and to the wrong person.

A secretary if she can rush out letters, last-minute notices, agendas and minutes, allowing judiciously for the vagaries of the postal services, attend all meetings, lend moral and practical support to her President, see the room from which she works in her home turned into a chaotic paper-chase — if she can cope with all that and not lose her head, then she can call herself a successful secretary, and pause to think back with admiration to Mrs. Nixon and Mrs. Young who single-handed were Secretaries bar none for the entire Association. And always now the Club Secretary has the District Secretary to turn to and the District Secretary the Association Secretary who knows all the answers. The direct limelight may not extend to encompass the Secretary, but generally speaking it is found she has no wish for it to do so, but like Mrs. Nixon and Mrs. Young, neither of whom ever became Association Presidents, is content to remain off-stage. If the organisation is served in this capacity tomorrow as well as it has been, its success will be due in great part to the Secretariat.

So Presidents and Secretaries have come and gone and fifty and more years have passed. And where do we go from here? Members engaged in the work of Extension of the movement will have looked in vain until now in this history for more than passing reference to their part in the scheme of things and have no doubt concluded they have been overlooked, but this is by no means the case. Theirs is indeed a special case and writing of their very real and vital role has been left deliberately until this point for it is essentially part of the future and so appears here in its rightful place.

In a sense the first Extension Chairman was the Founder herself. The first recorded meeting of Extension Officers as such, however, took place in the Russell Hotel, London in 1946. It has always been the policy of Inner Wheel not to have a Committee at Association level for the purpose of extending the movement but members elected to serve as Extension Chairmen or Organisers do have the opportunity to meet at the Annual Assembly, there to receive guidance from the Immediate Past President of the Association who is in the best possible position to direct and advise in the matter.

It has been seen how in every case Districts have grown in Great Britain and Ireland, how some have divided of themselves and therefore the number of them has multiplied. It is a success story of monumental proportions and proudly can be written of, but for the member personally involved in future growth, the pitfall of over-zealousness is omnipresent. 'Let us not go out for mere numerical strength,' warned Association President Jessie Park in 1949. 'Quality in membership is so much more important. Even if we cannot claim one hundred per cent Rotarian representation, in our Clubs we can aim at one hundred per cent active membership.' On the other hand at time of writing (but not necessarily at time of reading) there are upwards of one thousand and two hundred Rotary Clubs in Great Britain and Ireland and some nine hundred and seventy Inner Wheel Clubs and so there is still some way to go.

Considered advisable that an interval of three months should elapse before any initial approach to a new Rotary Club be made by Inner Wheel, this would seem to be reasonable, but should Inner Wheel be contacted before that time is up, then assuredly interest is strong enough for the Extension representative to welcome the overture and she is within her rights to go into action. She, of anyone, is the P.R.O. for the movement, must project the correct image, put over a clear picture to Rotarians and their ladies of what Inner Wheel is all about, and having done so, must patiently leave the final decision to those concerned, for never has there been any mind-bending or coercion employed. In small townships many are the calls made upon the same womenfolk to serve their communities. Understandably they can feel 'put upon' if already heavily committed in other organisations, when it is suggested to them they do more. The wise Extension Officer for Inner Wheel underlines that any *giving* is primarily of friendship and service, not money.

Once formed, very few Inner Wheel Clubs have 'folded'. Up until 1976 the figure was less than fifty. When that was announced then, at the Annual Conference it must have afforded members responsible for Extension in the past great satisfaction for it proved that they had made the move to form Clubs at the right time and in the right manner. 'Were I to know the world might perish tomorrow, I would still plant my apple tree today,' wrote Martin Luther — a challenging sentiment for District Extension Chairmen and Organisers. The movement is vigorous and the growth potential is still there to be explored. There is every hope of a positive future, but it would, of course, be presumptuous and foolhardy to assume any knowledge of what lies ahead for Inner Wheel, useless to indulge in any crystal-ball gazing, but taking into account its rapid growth, as outlined in 'Yesterday', and the unquestioned strength of its structure now, as explained in 'Today', it is surely consistent to expect great things of it.

Whereas this history is not intended to be a pious memorial to the work of Inner Wheel in Great Britain and Ireland, there have been moments of great triumph of which the usage of the cliché 'justly proud' is difficult to avoid. Corporate efforts, dating from the first years of World War II included that of presenting an Ambulance to the Red Cross in 1940. (The actual presentation took place in London at short notice and so only members of No. 13 District attended.) There followed the presentation of a Mobile Snack Bar by Association President Mrs. L. W. Barnard to Lady Iris Capell of the W.V.S. In 1943 a cheque for a substantial amount was handed over to Lady Cripps for the 'Women of China Fund' and in 1944 a cheque for an even greater sum was donated to the 'Merchant Navy Rescue Kit Fund'.

With the war over, effort was directed in 1946 into other

channels and the 'Save the Children Fund' received considerable financial support, after which Clubs reverted to giving to their local charities for a while. To commemorate the Silver Jubilee of the Association in 1959, however, an outstanding effort was made again by all, this for the British Empire Cancer Campaign. The figure of over £47,000 was reached and was used for the purchase of scientific apparatus in hospitals and laboratories throughout the country. All Districts had contributed, including some from overseas, and the scene was a touching one as each District Chairman in turn proffered to Lady Dorothy Macmillan, wife of the Prime Minister, a blue leather purse containing her District's total. Later in the Conference proceedings Sir Charles Lidbury, Honorary Treasurer of the British Empire Cancer Campaign, spoke warmly of the effort and thanked the Association for *the largest contribution of its kind ever received.*

After that gigantic endeavour it would have been excusable if Districts had rested on their laurels for a time, but 1960 was 'World Refugee Year', and although strictly speaking the effort made for this could not be classed as a corporate one, as monies raised were disbursed in the main to local charities, contributions from all Clubs went on record, and the total surpassed all previous ones, the figure reached well over £60,000. Down the years too, there have been many illustrious occasions in the Association's history to provide members with beautiful memories; among them the thrill when seats were allocated to the Association at the Coronation in 1953; the Association's own 'Coming of Age' Annual Conference in 1955, the church service at this held in St. Martin-in-the-Fields, the Reception in the Royal Festival Hall — the only Inner Wheel Conference ever to be held in London; attendance at the Conferences of other women's organisations; at Royal Garden Parties and Women of the Year Luncheons.

It is pleasing for members to be so recognised and gratifying for the Association as a whole, but people who look back too often are prone to fall over. Certainly it is desirable to preserve such memories and catalogue outstanding, morale-boosting successes, but to place too great a significance upon them is to stand still and no organisation can afford the luxury of doing that. Inner Wheel in Great Britain and Ireland has not done so. Basically and structurally it may not have changed despite change having been the dominant factor in life in these islands in the past fifty years, but it has *progressed*. Represented on most women's organisations at one time or another, including the W.R.V.S. on which it is still represented, Inner Wheel is now granted representation on the Women's National Commission, set up in 1969 by direct request of the Prime Minister as an advisory group to the Government on all controversial matters relating to women. The Association has, therefore, a voice at top level and faithful reportage of the Commission's meetings has become a regular item of Council business. This bodes well for the future for it puts the organisation in the strongest possible position to make its presence felt and the views of its members known to optimum effect.

To build Inner Wheel into what it is today has not been easy. If it appears its promotion has been effortless, it is because determinedly the happier moments in its history have been spotlighted. In reality it has called for dedicated application, self-sacrifice, endurance and much personal courage. Anyone whose membership takes them back only a few years can recall the senseless outrage which was perpetrated in the District of the Association President of 1972/73, which left her bereft of a beloved son, yet how that President continued in her service to become President of International Inner Wheel in the following year. All know of like fortitude displayed at Club and District level. In no way immune from the suffering and grief which touches all, many are the Inner Wheel members who are known to have taken office and held to it, as to a lifeline, in the face of personal calamity. In service they found an incentive, in Inner Wheel friendship a solace, and if the movement was never to accomplish aught else, that in itself has been worth while.

And if membership can scarcely be offered as a recipe for longevity, tragedy being no respecter of time or the individual, it is at least a source of wonder, glancing back a long way in this history for the last time, to discover the quite astonishing number of octogenarian and nonagenarian members who still today are taking part in the activities of their Inner Wheel

Clubs, some of whom remember Mrs. Golding clearly even now, and who greatly value having known her. There has even been one legendary figure, a Founder President of a Founder Club (Mrs. H. Garland of the Norwich Club, No. 8 District) who is known to have given a garden party for Past Presidents of her Club to celebrate her hundredth birthday, regularly attended the Annual Rotary Family Luncheon when in her hundreds, and at the age of one hundred and three made her last public appearance at her Club's fortieth anniversary. Exceptional cases perhaps, but interest sustained into such advanced years would seem to suggest that the sense of 'belonging' engendered by membership may have had a certain therapeutic value and in service these long and useful lives have been given purpose and direction.

In her address to the Annual Conference in 1971 Association President Mrs. M. Bulpitt, whose lively approach to her duties disguised a deep, underlying thoughtfulness, crystallised the essence of Inner Wheel by the relevant inclusion of a verse by Hilaire Belloc, much quoted ever since throughout the Districts —

'From quiet homes and first beginnings
Out to the undiscovered ends
There's nothing worth the wear of winning
But laughter and the love of friends.'

When it is remembered that those homes were homes in this country, those first beginnings were nurtured in these islands, grew, prospered and have reached out to form a sisterhood of friendship and service throughout the world, the Association of Inner Wheel Clubs in Great Britain and Ireland can be truly proud.

The times have never been more sympathetic to women. The world listens to them now. Their contribution to the management of world affairs becomes daily greater and that of Inner Wheel, marching with Rotary as it has always done, close to the ideology of that great movement, although separate from it will, there can be little doubt, as time passes, merit like recognition as a power force for the common good, for there is scarcely a facet of need or deprivation to which it has not already subscribed.

Inner Wheel has always scorned pretension in any form. The Constitution contains no official jargon. Any literature appertaining to it is couched in simple terms for no purpose has ever been served by pomposity, or indeed unnecessary solemnity. That is why this history has been written in as lighthearted a vein as was possible, why inclusion of dry as dust statistics has been kept to a minimum, for many of these by the time they are written, or read, are of no practical use to anyone, and Inner Wheel, it is hoped, has always been practical.

It is a history written in a small defiance of the gloom and doom merchants of today's world, for it is a *success* story, written by women, for women, about women, not famous or outstanding women, merely women who throughout half a century have made friendship their target nationally and internationally, which must have furthered world-wide under-standing in some measure.

Let the future look after itself is not a tenet held by any true Inner Wheel member. Individually and sincerely each is deeply concerned that tomorrow be a finer time in which to live. They may not consciously think of the services they give so piously. In fact, few if any, ever do. Nevertheless, past members have proved themselves to be forward-looking, *caring* people. Present members are proving it daily and the fate of the movement tomorrow lies not in the hands of any Association of it, nor in those of its Officers, nor in its Districts, nor even in its Clubs, but in you — and you — and you — the member who is reading this book and who, it is devoutly to be hoped, will feel inspired throughout all the years of her membership —

TO PROMOTE TRUE FRIENDSHIP

TO ENCOURAGE THE IDEALS OF PERSONAL SERVICE

TO FOSTER INTERNATIONAL UNDERSTANDING.